BUILDING BIGGER PEOPLE

BUILDING BIGGER PEOPLE

Success is more than numbers

John Glass

Authentic

MILTON KEYNES • COLORADO SPRINGS • HYDERABAD

14 13 12 11 10 09 08   8 7 6 5 4 3 2 1

This edition published 2008 by Authentic Media
9 Holdom Avenue, Bletchley, Milton Keynes, MK1 1QR, UK
1820 Jet Stream Drive, Colorado Springs, CO 80921, USA
OM Authentic Media, Medchal Road, Jeedimetla Village,
Secunderabad 500 055, A.P., India
www.authenticmedia.co.uk

Authentic Media is a division of IBS-STL U.K., limited by guarantee, with its
Registered Office at Kingstown Broadway, Carlisle, Cumbria CA3 0HA.
Registered in England & Wales No. 1216232. Registered charity 270162

British Library Cataloguing in Publication Data
A catalogue record for this book is available from the British Library

ISBN-13: 978-1-85078-776-1

Cover Design by fourninezero design.
Print Management by Adare
Printed in Great Britain by J.H. Haynes & Co., Sparkford

To the tens of thousands of Elim people around the world, our pastors and leaders – and especially my friends on Elim's National Leadership Team without whose encouragement and support I would not have been able to fulfil my ministry.

Contents

Acknowledgements   ix
Foreword by Colin Dye   xi
Introduction   xv

1. The Flavour of Favour   1
2. The Four-faced Church   14
3. A Bigger Voice   48
4. Generational Blessing   81
5. The Home of the Heart   89
6. Space for Grace   122
7. Stepping Up   146

Epilogue   162
Notes   164

Acknowledgements

My thanks to Charlotte Hubback of Authentic Media for her comments on the manuscript. This book has greatly benefitted from her input and advice. Thanks too to John Martin for the part he played in the production of the cover design.

Foreword

The Church of today is facing challenges from the increasing secularisation of society and from aggressive religious efforts to replace Christianity as the dominant religious influence in the west. The mass media draws attention to dwindling numbers in churches and reports almost daily on the institutional ineffectiveness of Christianity. And yet, to paraphrase Mark Twain, reports of this death have been greatly exaggerated. The Church in Britain is alive and well! Not only is there a significant number of growing churches which are engaging with their communities in relevant and effective service, but society as a whole is still leaning towards its Christian tradition. The government census of 2001 showed that 72 per cent of people in the nation identified themselves with the Christian faith.

One of the most urgent tasks we face is to help this silent majority rediscover the vital and personal element of faith in Christ and to disciple them into congregational and community life. In our generation as in every other, the Church is the only answer to the needs of the nation. We have the message of life in the gospel of Jesus which is the only hope for damaged individuals, families and communities.

George Jeffries, the founder of the Elim Movement, blazed a trail for Christ during the depressed and inauspicious conditions of Britain almost a century ago. Now, evangelical believers and Pentecostal churches such as Elim are on the move again. John Glass has been leading the Elim Movement for the better part of the last decade and has inspired a new generation of Elim people with the vision that things can be different and that we can bring a vibrant, relevant and effective Christian witness to contemporary society. His emphasis has been on 'building bigger people' and this goes to the heart of the New Testament mandate. It is not a 'new' revelation. Jesus set this paradigm in motion from the very beginning. He said, '*I* will build my Church – you make disciples.' (Mt. 16:18)

And yet John Glass' reminder is timely. Today we are fond of one-stop solutions, we look for the easy answer and we search for techniques to produce successful churches and rapid growth. This has led to successive 'solutions' being touted to British churches with the attendant hype and glib promises of a quick answer. Often from abroad, these methodologies deliver little by way of long-term results and the fallout is extensive. Young pastors today are disillusioned with such 'secrets of success' promising everything and delivering nothing. They long for something deeper, more meaningful and above all authentic.

Sound in biblical principles, rich in practical application and steeped in personal experience, *Building Bigger People* takes us forward in the journey of recovery towards this much sought-after authenticity. Far from the personality driven, superstar approach to which much Pentecostal and charismatic Christianity has succumbed in recent years, John Glass takes us back to the original task of the Church – focussing on people, and, beginning with ourselves, building character and shaping personality into the image of Jesus. Initially, this process, by its very nature, will produce nothing by way of spectacular results. But in the long run these principles will bring us closer to what Jesus had in mind when he commissioned the Church to win the world. I am delighted that John Glass has committed to print his teaching on this vital issue making it available, not only to Elim people, but also to the wider body of Christ.

Colin Dye
Senior Pastor, Kensington Temple

Introduction

Fifty years ago the Christian Church embarked on a voyage of self-examination. It has scrutinised forms of worship, models of leadership and, in some quarters, the question has even been asked if the gathered congregation should continue at all in its present form.

While it is essential that we should continually appraise ourselves, an obsession with analysis generally leads to immobility. When the centipede, who previously had no problem at all in walking, was asked which of his hundred legs he started out on each day, he was thrown into such confusion that he found himself totally incapacitated – unable to proceed at all.

The lack of growth of the Church in Europe can be blamed on a variety of spiritual viruses across the continent. Currently in the United Kingdom fifty thousand sermons are preached every week resulting in two thousand decisions – never to attend church again!

Blame is often put at the door of the increasingly militant secular fundamentalist politicians who seek to marginalise – even eradicate – Christianity from the agenda of public life. Those within both politics and the media continually talk tolerance – with the apparent caveat that everything should be tolerated except the person who declares themself to be a committed Christian.

While not denying these factors, and sometimes having publicly contended for their veracity myself, it has to be said that part of the perceived demise of the Church is down to a misalignment of its own focus that has resulted in an ensuing identity crisis.

It is disingenuous of the Church to present itself as a victim. We in the west have not even begun to understand what real persecution means.

The underground church in China has reached an estimated eighty million with little or no hierarchical structures or chain of command. This point is made not to denigrate structure, for there can be inherent weaknesses in poor systemic shape, but China serves to show that growth can still occur even where an ideal infrastructure is not in place.

Those who are really suffering include the tens of thousands who are caught up in the genocide in the Sudan directed mainly at the Christian Church. The horrors perpetrated in North Korea also bring into sharp perspective a context of protracted pain.

Churches divide and split over minutiae. Sections of the Church insist, lemming-like, on chasing mice while lions are destroying the land and painting the fence while the house is on fire.

In a previous book, *Open Heart Open Hands*, I drew attention to the apparent proclivity of denominations to become stuck in a time warp that often correlates with the period in which they had formerly know their greatest power. This sense of dominance may be reflected in political supremacy for the established churches or a pinnacle of growth for the newer churches. This can be seen in the medieval music and vestments in one group, eighteenth-century hymns in another or gospel music reminiscent of the 1950s in another section.

In many churches there is a healthy eclecticism that can draw from the best of all.

The problem arises when one group or another concludes that their forms – be it music, liturgy or church structures – are God's final word to contemporary ecclesiology or that their wineskins, old or new, reflect a superior spirituality.

Big People cannot be confined to such straitjackets or embalmed in the sepia nostalgia of the 'good old days'.

Some, like Peter on the Mount of Transfiguration, want to build a booth to preserve the sense of God's glory by stopping the clock in a period of particular blessing. Another radical view is that the Church should be deconstructed into its lowest common denominator and, on many occasions where this has been attempted, finds itself evaporated into the ether.

What we can be sure of is that the Church as it is expressed today is, in many cases, a pale parody of what it was in New Testament times and certainly of what it should be.

Richard Halverson, when Chaplain of the United States Senate is quoted in *Leadership* magazine, volume 19, as saying that the Church began as a fellowship of men and women centred on Jesus. It went to Greece and became a philosophy. It went to Rome and became an institution. It went to Europe and became a culture and then to America to become an enterprise.

The well-intentioned Church Growth Movement wrestling with spiritual market forces towards the close of the twentieth century encouraged us to set targets. This, it was thought, would spur leaders and congregations alike out of their perceived complacency. People soon became disillusioned. No one doubted the motive but disenchantment quickly followed. The problem with disillusionment is not that people are sad at having failed but that they become de-motivated from ever trying again.

There is only so much hype that people can endure. It's a little like the member of a congregation that has listened to a succession of pastors that have come and gone each appearing to promise a panacea that will cure all ills if only 'the vision can be caught'. Though vision is essential to both effective leadership and development, not all 'vision' emanates out of leaders seeking the mind of God for the key to the community context. Much of it may; but too much of it does not.

Concepts imported from other cultures are almost always incompatible with the way church runs elsewhere; in the same way that most Apple programmes will not work on a PC. It is not that that the operating systems are intrinsically wrong, it is simply that you cannot just download software indiscriminately, and expect it to work on every platform.

There can be no doubt that the siren sounds of ecclesiastical bandwagons are alluring and their capacity for seduction should not be underestimated. The core of their influence feeds on frustration. For the terminally frustrated, there has to be an answer, a blueprint, a silver bullet that will find the bull's-eye and prove to themselves that they are on target.

When statistical objectives alone are our criteria of success we encounter a plethora of pitfalls – the two most serious being a departure from a biblical mandate and the creating of a flawed benchmark by which to critique success both on an individual level and in the local church.

I am conscious of the fact that there are three books in the Old Testament that devote themselves largely to the gathering of statistical data. I am also aware that in the New Testament Jesus clearly expressed to his disciples that the reason why they had been called was to 'bring forth fruit'. But this was not just the fruit that could be counted, weighed and displayed. It was 'fruit that will last'.

It is little use having a Church that is a thousand kilometres wide and only a few centimetres deep. That is why the Great Commission is about making disciples rather than converts.

Some years ago I was speaking for my good friend Luke Brough who pastors the Auckland Elim Church, one of the largest congregations of any denomination in New Zealand. In a break between the meetings he suggested that we go down to the harbour to see the boats that had gathered for the America's Cup.

The first thing that struck me was how close we were able to get to the yachts and also how little security there appeared to be. After all, the pride of nations depended on the outcome of the race.

A few moments later our attention was drawn to a flurry of activity a few hundred metres away. It transpired that one of the vessels was being lifted by crane from the water; we assumed for repair. Immediately the security that I had considered to be absent kicked in as curtains were drawn around the boat – not around the sail or the deck, but the keel.

As we should have realised, the secret of sailing success does not just depend upon the expertise of the crew or the shape of the hull. It is primarily about the design of the keel. What was above the waterline was less important that what lay beneath the surface. It was the 'invisibles' that made the difference between victory and failure.

There was a time that if anyone had challenged me to measure the height of a tree, I would have instinctively started from the ground up. Not any more. The size of the tree should be calculated from the lowest tap root to the highest branch.

Paul Yonghi Cho once told of how he had become perpetually frustrated with the traffic congestion around a building site in the city centre en route to his church complex. The problem was not that construction was taking place, but that so little progress seemed to have been made week by week. There were security screens the other side of which could be heard the noise of activity and the rattle of pneumatic drills, but nothing appeared to materialise as a consequence of the clamour. Pulling his car over, he approached one of the workers to ask what was happening, and was told that they were concentrating all their efforts on the foundations. 'Because we intend to build big we have to ensure that we dig deep.'

God is not against 'Big'. God loves 'Big' and has called his Church to largeness, favour and growth. But if there is one thing that God prioritises over 'Big' in the economy of his kingdom, it is 'Deep'.

That is what this book is about. It is not about seven steps to success or how to build a bigger church. It is about how to build a Bigger People for, as we shall discover on our journey together, Bigger People can be entrusted with bigger blessings, greater responsibilities, larger challenges and, eventually greater success – success that lasts.

I have written several books but I have yet to pen anything that I feel is as important as the principles that we will be sharing in the following pages. The fact that you have selected this title means that there is something that has already quickened your step to embark on a voyage – a voyage that we will take together in the chapters that are to come.

1

The Flavour of Favour

Christians continually pray for 'blessing' for ourselves, our families, our friends and our church. Blessing is not the most specific of words and notoriously hard to define. It seems to imply an overall awareness of well-being. It certainly carries with it a sense of spiritual prosperity, whatever that means: and that's the problem. When we pray for 'those in authority over us', whether that means people in politics or our local pastor, it's quite difficult at the end of the day to say whether or not our prayers have been answered, as the term is too nebulous. It is not specific enough. If we are honest we all do it and it is, without doubt, a lazy way of praying.

The dictionary offers a definition as, 'The bestowal of divine favour.' That's certainly a good place to start.

If friends ask us how our church is doing we might reply that it is currently experiencing a 'time of blessing'. That in itself could mean one of two things. It might refer to what we might call 'postcard blessing', the kind of thing we write to people when we are on holiday and which amounts to, 'Having a great time, wish you were here.' There is nothing intrinsically wrong with that of course for it is far better to speak in those terms than, 'It's totally miserable where we are worshipping, you should be glad you are well out of it.' The problem is that 'postcard' blessing is as transient as the vacation that is all too quickly followed by a Monday morning back at work in the real world.

Blessing that carries substance emanates out of a sense of favour that percolates through to the place where our destiny is affected and spills over into our long-term future. It speaks of foundational impact and radical change.

The well-rounded word, 'Shalom', with its sense of wholeness that permeates body, soul and spirit is the most applicable.

Bigger People, who live with a sense of wholeness, are capable of handling bigger challenges that lead to greater opportunities of ministry and service.

It is sometime said that, 'God can use anybody.' Well, if he can, it is very evident that he doesn't. God rarely entrusts big responsibility to small minds and timid hearts. What he does do is to commence with those of us who identify our weakness and allow the Holy Spirit to challenge our faith to grow to the place where the altar of our life is large enough to place a sacrifice that is worth giving. We start with smallness – move to enlargement – and then on to an understanding that God fills every vacuum that we are willing to surrender to him.

The tragedy with the Church is that it tends to swing to one of two extremes. It either denigrates or exalts itself beyond any chance of usefulness.

All twelve spies that went into Canaan saw huge giants and tall walls. The difference between Caleb and Joshua and the rest was not what they saw but how they saw themselves. In Numbers 13:33 it records that the ten said, 'We seemed like grasshoppers in our eyes.' It is important that we note that they did not say that they seemed to the giants to be grasshoppers but that they considered themselves to be grasshoppers.

On the other hand, there are those who God blesses with enlargement who then become conceited and so expel themselves from any possibility of spiritual expansion.

'Jeshuran grew fat and kicked . . . He abandoned the God who made Him'.[1] One translation (TEV) says, 'The Lord's people grew rich but rebellious.'

This always occurs at the point that we arrive at a conclusion that favour is solely for our own soul and forget that we are blessed to be a blessing. This is true whether the favour we experience is financial or concerns the development of our personal ministry and gifts.

Until we are big enough to receive, God will not be able to bless us to the capacity of the abundance that is part of our potential pre-ordained inheritance.

Some may struggle with any sense of a God who is 'not able'. But the Scriptures make it abundantly clear that God chooses to confine himself in many situations to the level of the faith that we elect to exercise. Even to the degree that when giving an account of his visit to one town it is reported that, 'He could not do any miracles there, except lay his hands on a few sick people and heal them. And he was amazed at their lack of faith.'[2]

But it is not just lack of faith that impedes accelerated favour, it is also lack of growth.

In the days of Moses the people had been given the promise of territorial blessing and were on course to move into their possession. There was, however, an unprecedented hurdle that they faced in the account recorded in Exodus 23.

God was prepared to drive out their enemies before them but was forced to change gear downwards as far as the timescale was concerned. Their enemies were one problem and the wild animals in the area were another. To get rid of their enemies would only launch another, different, dilemma on the people of God. As a result, the word that came to Moses was, 'Little by little I will drive them out before you until you have increased enough to take possession of the land.' The issue, once again, was 'until you are big enough'.[3]

There are two kind of favour that the believer encounters. We will call them first and second-level favour.

First-level favour occurs at the point we become a Christian and are born again. This favour springs from grace and is a free gift of God which cannot be either earned or deserved. Paul writes to the Ephesians and says, 'By grace you have been saved through faith . . . not of works so that no man can boast.'[4]

If you are reading this and are a child of God you have already experienced this favour for yourself.

Second-level favour comes as a result of our actions and depends upon what we do or don't do. The positive thing about this is that we can grow into it – the negative thing is that we can step out of it.

It is important to sound a note of caution at this point. This does not mean that if you are experiencing apparently negative things in your life as you are reading this that therefore you are necessarily living wrongly or that there is sin in your life.

Some of the greatest Christians I have known have undergone trials and tests – the reasons for which are incomprehensible this side of heaven. There are also Christians suffering unimaginable persecution in the Muslim and communist worlds whose godly lifestyle would put most of us to shame.

Hebrews 11 paints a picture of heroes of the faith who fall into two distinct categories. One group are miraculously delivered from torture and threat while the other experiences death as martyrs. The writer makes it clear that neither faith nor spiritual growth is the issue. It was simply a matter of the purpose of God and, in the case of those who suffered most, refers to them as those, 'of whom the world was not worthy'.

Having said that, in a general sense, second-level favour can be both sought and lost – it can be entered into and exited from.

Favour is about 'growth' and favour is about 'place'.

Hannah had longed for a child for years and, when God eventually granted her request, she handed him back to God and he served in the temple of the Lord. Each year she visited him and every time she came she brought the same present – a bigger robe.[5]

He was a growing boy. He was getting bigger and yesterday's mantle, though right for that period in his development, would become a restricting straitjacket unless he was given the opportunity to expand into a new and bigger garment. A loving mother saw that.

Yet it was not just his physique that was developing. His character was growing too, as was his relationship and confidence in God: 'The boy Samuel continued to grow in stature and in favour with the Lord and with men.'[6]

There are two embracing arms that extend to draw God's favour towards the Church. The first is intimacy and the second integrity.

The Arm of Intimacy

In Exodus 33 God says to Moses, 'I know you by name and you have found favour with me.'

It is possible to own an umbrella and still get wet. 'Keeping dry' is not about ownership but about sheltering securely in a safe place. That God has made things available to us does not necessarily mean that we are 'in a place' where his best blessings are consistently being experienced by us.

The prodigal was loved by his father just as much when he was in the pig pen and away from home as in the days when he sat in the comfort and luxury of the family home. The issue was not the place that he had in his father's heart but the place to which he had chosen to remove himself.

One afternoon, when I was preparing to bring the final message at our Bible Week in the Big Top at Butlins Minehead, I was disturbed by a strange sound outside my chalet.

Looking through the glass door I discovered a pair of ducks that had come looking for food. There they were, pecking the window and as soon as my wife saw them she immediately started to search for some bread for them.

Two minutes earlier we had been thinking of neither ducks nor bread but these simple creatures had instinctively learned by experience that if they roam from chalet to chalet making quacking noises and looking cute, there was a fair chance that someone would take pity on them and provide them with what might pass for a meal. Though not the most intelligent of creatures, they had discovered that favour was connected with 'place'.

The birds were satisfied with begging for scraps. As the children of God, scraps are not our inheritance. The Scriptures says that, a million miles away from a meagre meal, we are taken into God's banqueting hall and his banner over us is his love[7] – not pity nor condescension.

As Jesus surveyed the hapless inhabitants of Jerusalem, and saw them as sheep without a shepherd, he also called up another ornithological illustration when he expressed that he longed to gather them all as a hen gathers its chicks under its wings.[8]

Coming close means intimacy, intimacy leads to shelter and shelter is part, as we shall see later, of God's favour.

The Arm of Integrity

'Noah found favour in the eyes of the LORD . . . Noah was a righteous man.'[9]

I would not want to live in a construction where the builders had failed to use a spirit-level and, in the same way, I would not want to be part of a Church that fails to apply the Holy Spirit level to calibrate the stages of its development.

These are days in which God is putting his plumb-line against his Church. Sadly there are areas of Christendom that are failing to apply a biblical yardstick but are electing instead to employ the crooked criteria of a fallen world. They measure their world-view against acceptable social convention and political correctness – concepts that too often emanate from the very politicians and secular fundamentalists who, if they had their way, would attempt to marginalise the Church to the hinterland of insignificance.

Bigger People will not allow themselves to be bullied into subservience to the state when the state avows principles that cut across the clear teaching of biblical truth – nor will it allow their children to be indoctrinated by a perverse and perverted view of God's world.

The vast majority of the Christians that I know are neither in rebellion against God nor engaging in sin from which they refuse to be free. Like the rest of us they are on a journey. They have moved radically from a life lived for themselves and are seeking, by God's grace, to live for him in an expression of their faith that means that they also wish to live with a focus on others.

The average Christian probably does not consider themselves to be on a spiritual plane where favour is to be expected. Favour is not for them but for some perceived elite that shares the limelight on an ecclesiastical stage that is beyond their reach. Others may even consider it pretentious or selfish to ask anything for themselves – all the time failing to realise that it is out of the overflow of what God does for them that he chooses to bless the lives of others.

Yet another category embraces a vocabulary of emotional asceticism; the favourite word of which is emptiness. Theirs is a worm-theology that categorises themselves as dust and nothingness; falsely, though often sincerely, believing that this attitude is actually a manifestation of humility.

Bigger People realise that in themselves, and depending on their natural strength gifts and talents, they are inadequate. But they don't stay there. They have also come to realise that by seeking a place of favour, and by setting themselves with a determination to grow, they can in fact increase their capacity to receive. Their goal is not enlargement for its own sake but neither do they have any desire to deteriorate into stagnant pools that take in but have no outlet. These people long to be a tributary: a spiritual conduit that, by continually living in fullness, can be a source of irrigation into the desert place. Those arid areas may include the sink estates that house a marginalised and disempowered underclass at the lowest strata of the socio-economic pecking order. It might equally be in the area amid the vacuous vanity of those steeped in a materialistic culture that, while cash rich, is emotionally starved.

Periodically, sections of the Church become frustrated with the ineffectualness of the ecclesiastical establishment to provide an answer and commence a group that they believe is expressing a purer or more developed expression of how the Church should be.

The small band of men and women who, a century ago, pioneered the Elim Movement that I currently have the privilege of leading had no ambition to commence a new denomination. On the contrary, their heart was to bring the message, of what they believed to be the full gospel, to a world which for the most part was denying the miraculous and unwilling to embrace the gifts of the Spirit.

The many thousands of people who aligned themselves to this new move of the Spirit were not made welcome by the establishment. As so often is the case whenever a lost emphasis is brought to the attention of the Church, there are always those who choose to recoil from a newly highlighted doctrine and feel the need to pigeon-hole both the messengers and the message. They appear to need to put those that they cannot understand at arm's length and draw a convenient perimeter around them in an attempt to sanitise them to a safe distance. All of us are in danger of taking a similar stance. Its roots are in insecurity and it is a tendency that we should do out best to resist.

Those who did embrace the message were often ejected from the churches they attended. A larger group, who previously had had no church affiliation of any kind, but had experienced new birth subsequent to hearing the gospel, sought to continue fellowship with those who had first introduced them to Christ. The appellation 'Pentecostal', as if this was the only doctrine they taught, soon stuck.

Those now left with the responsibility of pastoring and discipling the thousands of people who were part of this new movement, looked for a name that would best reflect what they believed God wanted this new stream to be. Our sister Fellowship choose the name Assemblies of God – the nearest thing to 'Church' that they could find to express who they wanted to be. The group to which I belong were named Elim. The founder, George Jeffreys, took the name from an oasis that the children of Israel come across during their journeying. It was a place where they found twelve wells of water that provided refreshment for the twelve tribes and also palm trees that proffered shelter and shade. In short, the pioneers of the modern Pentecostal Movement saw the world as a desert in which the Church should be an oasis of refreshing and shade.

Whatever contributes to the scorched earth of a godless culture – be it material, emotional or spiritual poverty – it is the Church that is called to address the issues. No single section of the Christian communion has the monopoly on either truth or the movement of the Spirit. All sections of the Church have things that they can teach to, and learn from, one another.

The most encouraging landmark on the ecclesiastical landscape as this book goes to print is the willingness of so many groups, whether they class themselves a denomination or not, to put kingdom before all other considerations. There is no better environment in which to live than where Christ is given his rightful place and the Holy Spirit, rather than sectarian party spirit, is the expressed essence of our energy.

Having said that, I do not see Church as divided into denominations but rather multiplied into them. Denominations should be a healthy and vibrant expression of the Church. I have always been passionate about the concept of denomination. Denominationalism, that is conceived out of schism and split and suckled by personal agendas and inflated egos, is incontrovertibly the work of the enemy.

Denominations themselves are a celebration of variety and very much part of God's order. God could have chosen to given the world a single variety of flower or a single breed of animal but chose to give us thousands of species instead. We could have inhabited a two-tone visual environment but instead have been allowed to enjoy a full spectrum of colour. One cannot help but be somewhat bemused at those who have spoken most vehemently about denominations and have then gone on to set up their own groups to prove a point that I think eludes most of us.

God never suggested in the Old Testament that the existence of Israel's tribes were an indictment against unity and should be therefore be disbanded. All were encouraged to rejoice in their loyalty to their respective banners. The cohesion came at the point that, when they camped, God specifically stipulated how they should do so. The most important factor was that it was the Tabernacle, that housed the special presence of God, that was always to be at their centre.

Were any of the tribes to position themselves into the place reserved for the glory of God it would have the effect of moving the hub from the centre of the wheel and invite disaster.

Many years ago I was talking on this subject with my good friend Paul Weaver, the current General Superintendent of the Assemblies of God in the UK, and he used the analogy of the jigsaw. His view was that most people look at the picture on the box and fill in the straight edges first: but straight edges are exclusive. His point was that the key to completion is that each piece has the capacity to contribute to the piece next to it and as well as receiving input from the part to which it connects.

God's view of his kingdom is bigger than ours and only he sees the full and comprehensive picture. Whichever denominations, streams or networks that we belong to should not fill in the straight edges. We should be available to interface with other expressions of Church to which we can be linked to fulfil God's mandate on the Earth.

Both Paul and I were close friends long before we were elected to lead our respective groups and we are sometimes asked why our two groups do not join one another given that the differences between us are administrative rather than doctrinal. Our answer is always the same. There is no need to merge structurally as on a heart basis we are already one.

The secular world is consumed with the idea of logo and brand. The concept commenced as farmers needed to identify their own animals and literally branded them with marks that differentiated one group from another. At a later stage goldsmiths would brand with a hallmark that went further and expressed, 'This is my work and I am proud to identify with it.' It did not say my hallmark is superior to anyone else's.

Bigger People are big enough to see the Church as larger than themselves. Unity with those of a like mind is so often a precursor to the unprecedented outpouring of the favour of God on a community – sometimes referred to by the over-used word 'revival'. There are a multitude of references to this throughout Church history apart from the many parallels that can be found within both the Old and New Testaments.

We shall return at a later point to the issue of why integrity is more than just choosing 'righteous options'.

Integrity is a vital and pivotal ingredient in the development of successful Christian living in a road pockmarked by hype, marketing and spin.

There are four things that the Scriptures reveal are the flavour of favour – something that the Christian should expect as their rightful inheritance.

PEACE

'Glory to God in the highest, and on earth peace to men on whom his favour rests.'[10]

PROTECTION

'For surely O LORD, you bless the righteous; you surround them with your favour as with a shield'[11]

'For the LORD God is a sun and shield; the LORD bestows favour and honour; no good thing does he withhold from those whose walk is blameless.'[12]

FREEDOM

'The Spirit of the Lord is on me, because he has anointed me to preach good news to the poor. He has sent me to proclaim freedom for the prisoners and recover of sight to the blind, to release the oppressed, to proclaim the year of the Lord's favour.'[13]

FULLNESS

'Naphtali is abounding with the favour of the Lord and is full of his blessing; he will inherit.'[14]

2

The Four-faced Church

The story is told of a couple who had invited a fellow church member around for a meal and excused themselves while they made last-minute preparations in the kitchen. The lady, who was known as being the source of some dissent in the church in the past, was left alone in the lounge for a while but was eventually joined by an inquisitive little boy who, without uttering a word, circumnavigated the visitor like a boat around a lighthouse.

The guest, feeling uncomfortable under the silent scrutiny, eventually asked what the little lad thought he was doing. 'Oh' said the boy innocently, 'I heard my Mummy and Daddy say earlier that they had invited a two-faced woman around for dinner, and I was just trying to find where the other one was.'

Two-faced is obviously not a good condition but, in the case of the Church, four-faced is perfect.

A reading of Ezekiel 1 reveals that Church with less than four faces fails to meet God's criteria as a powerful presence in the world.

There are elements in the chapter that may appear to be both strange and incongruous. It is said that the Jews considered the passage to be of such significance that there was a time when no man under a prescribed age was even allowed to read it – let alone delve into its interpretation and was cryptically referred to by the Rabbis as simply, 'The Matter of the Chariot.'

An objective observer could be mistaken in believing that the passage was in fact a description of a UFO given its references to wheels of glowing metal that darted to and fro amidst fire and which had 'eyes' around its rim. The allusion is compounded when Ezekiel says that emerging from the storm and wind that the vehicle evoked, came strange four-faced creatures.

These faces are remarkable for many reasons not least that they were also witnessed by Daniel and also by John on the Isle of Patmos some six hundred years later.[1] Each of them speak of seeing the remarkable portrayal before their eyes of the image of a lion, an ox, a man and an eagle.

Most commentators concur that the Old Testament visions were Christophanies – pre-incarnation manifestations of the nature of Christ. This has been deduced from the fact that the faces reveal the four facets of the revelation of the nature of Jesus as portrayed in the gospels.

Matthew consistently reveals Jesus as king (lion). The Sermon on the Mount is known as his manifesto and parables of the kingdom abound throughout the text. Mark emphasises Jesus as servant (ox); Luke as the Son of Man and John gives prominence in his writing to the divinity of Christ (eagle).

John is sometimes referred to as the 'beloved disciple' and the one who is perceived to be the closest to the Lord Jesus. Under normal circumstances, it is those who are the closest to us that are the more aware of our faults and the expressions of imperfection that only serve to amplify and underline our humanity. Yet it is this disciple, whose perspective arises out of the closest proximity to the Lord, who testifies the most ardently that Jesus was indeed the Son of God.

However, whatever exegetical tools are used to excavate the importance of Ezekiel 1, all are agreed that there is a desire by the inspirer of Scripture to grant us a spectacular glimpse of the glory of God.

Hunger for God's glory transcends time and culture. When Moses wanted to see it God responded by saying, 'I will cause all my goodness to pass before you'.[2] How that happened we are not told but it became clear to Moses, and now does so to us, that the manifestation of God's glory was far more than the existential experience of 'goosebumps down the spine'. It was about the strong spiritual substance of character.

When David wanted to experience this glory he found the definition eloquently articulated in God's creative power. Having his eyes lifted towards the grandeur of a night sky he writes, 'The heavens declare the glory of God.'[3]

For the apostle John, it was evident that the miracles of Jesus were a further expression of this. Referring to the first recorded miracle in which water was turned to wine he comments that the Lord, 'Thus revealed his glory'.[4]

Perhaps the most poignant parallel in a perception of what defines 'glory' in this context occurs just a few days before Calvary. In what has come to be known as the high-priestly prayer of Jesus, the disciples eavesdrop on his intercession to the Father as he announces, 'The glory that you have given me, I have given them.'[5]

From that moment on it was the Church that was to become the conduit of glory; be it manifest in character, the communication of the majesty of God or through miracles. It was then, and still remains, a huge mandate.

Like a mantle it rests on our shoulders. One-dimensional Church cannot do it. Only four-dimensional Church can.

The Face of an Eagle

Of the four creatures, the eagle is the only one that is not confined to earth and therefore retains a heavenly perspective. This is the highest priority for the Church. In the early part of my ministry I would have said that this 'face' designated spirituality, and when making that statement would consider spirituality as abstract in form, almost ethereal and usually linked to expressions of worship found in the gathered church or in private devotion.

Most of us have come to realise that spirituality cannot be compartmentalised. We cannot segregate what we do alone with God in prayer, and what we do in church on the weekend, from the rest of our lives. To make any sense at all, spirituality must percolate through marriage, business, recreation and be as evident in an evaluation of our bank statements as our doctrinal statements.

The essence of Bigger People is not that they live on a different plane. It is that their vision and dream cannot be confined to the naked eye but scans a landscape from a higher vantage point. By being interfaced to the infinite they come to realise that God's ways are always higher than our ways and his thoughts than our thoughts.[6]

This is not only true when trying to evaluate the bigger picture that we often associate with expansive faith. It is not just about the capacity to believe in instantaneous miracles: it is equally about how we handle life's challenges. A friend of mine who lectures at our college once commented to me that evangelicals, with their grasp of faith and forgiveness, have virtually no concept of the theology of suffering. In consequence, when bad things happen to good people, a retreat into a doctrine of denial is their only recourse.

The harrowing journey of Gladys Alward out of war-torn Yang Chen, and her heroic attempt to preserve the lives of the children in her charge, has been well documented. A pivotal point arises at a moment when she feels that the task is totally hopeless and she is at a loss to see any means of escape.

It is at that juncture, as she sits despairingly with her head in her hands, that she is approached by a young girl who says to her, 'Why are you crying? You mustn't forget the stories you told us about how God delivered Moses in the wilderness.'

Trying to remain tender and truthful at the same time the weary missionary is believed to have responded, 'Yes, my dear, but I am not Moses.'

'That is true,' retorted the young girl, 'But God is still God.'

The perception of the eagle declares God to be God in every situation because it acknowledges that the finite mind is an inadequate mechanism with which to understand the infinite. In such situations it is only the heavenly perspective that can be trusted.

When Isaiah spoke about a 'valley of vision'[7] it seemed like a contradiction in terms. The reality however is that – wherever we find ourselves geographically and however our 'position' is mapped in health, wealth, home or church – God's satellite navigation will always log us in to his way out. There are no cul-de-sacs with him. The one who opened the Red Sea can most certainly find a door out of every prison we face into the destiny that has been charted for us. That is why we believe that, 'In all things God works for the good of those who love him, who have been called according to his purpose.'[8]

Some may find the old cliché trite that says, 'When the outlook is bad try the up look', but this is exactly what David did when surrounded by the desertion of those who had previously supported him. His only resort was to, 'encourage himself in the Lord.'[9]

A lot of my time is spent in planes. Travelling in daylight at thirty thousand feet the sky is always blue. However, there are many occasions when the pilot announces that we are shortly to land into a host air-port that he describes in terms of darkness, wind and rain. Its hard to imagine that things are going to be so different 'down there' but the descent soon indicates how accurate the pilot was. Earth's atmosphere is light years away from the ambience of heaven. That is why it is only God's perspective that can truly be trusted.

In the days when air travel was in its infancy, and most planes were constructed of wood and seated only the pilot, the ailerons that controlled the wings were controlled by cables rather than electronically as they are today.

The story is told of a pilot who noticed a grating sound as he was flying solo high above a wide expanse of water. Turning around he saw to his horror that a rat, which had entered the aircraft prior to take-off, was suc-cessfully gnawing through one of the crucial cords. He was suddenly aware that in minutes his plane would be completely out of control and would consequently crash. As there was nowhere for him to land it seemed inevitable that his fate had been sealed and he was about to die.

It was then that he realised that he possessed something that the rat did not: a supply of oxygen. He survived by climbing to an altitude where he could exist and the rat could not.

There is a place there for all of us. The eagle knows its location. It is her habitat.

Neither are divine vantage points there for our benefit alone. They are there so that we can occupy a place of intercession on behalf of others. Intercession is most used in the context of prayer but it is not limited to it. By seeking God on behalf of others we are enabled through the Gifts of the Spirit to gain an understanding of issues that we had not naturally known and to impart wisdom beyond ourselves.

Many fine Christians, whose theology may not precisely parallel with my own, will be able to recount from their own experience instances when God has granted a level of revelation and understanding that transcends the natural and caused them to connect with situations of which they could not have previously been cognisant. The preacher finds themself communicating in the context of a message things that had not been previously prepared. There comes a flow that some might designate as being a special anointing and others as prophetic. The semantics are superfluous and simply do not matter. The reality is that heaven is touching earth in a special way. The eagle has landed.

It was P.T. Forsyth who said, 'You must live with people to know their problems and with God to know how to solve them.'

Higher perspective has to be the habitation of those who aspire to be Bigger People. Not only does it affect the realm of intercession but assists us in countering the numbing effects of intimidation over our lives.

In my formative years as a pastor I embarked on my first ministry trip to the USA. When it concluded, and prior to leaving for home and flying out of one of the major airports, I was taken for lunch by the pastor of the large church I had been currently speaking at and who was accompanied by two businessmen from his congregation that he introduced to me as being multimillionaires.

During the course of the meal they described the nature of their business and the size of their companies. One of them illustrated this by pointing out of the window to two skyscrapers he owned. I had no sense that they were boasting. They were simply being real about who they were. As a young man I remember my awe at their success and felt somewhat small. Any sense of intimidation I felt however arose solely out the mindset of someone who was not used to mixing with those who I considered to be giants of industry.

Later, as my plane took off, I reflected on the encounter while, at the same time, gazing out at the very buildings that had earlier loomed so large when I saw them through the window of the restaurant. As the plane continued to gain height, the skyscrapers were reduced to the size of matchboxes and before long became no more than dots on a wide horizon. What had previously intimidated me was now far beneath my feet not because they had physically diminished but because I had altered my perspective.

When the Church regains its confidence to challenge the false suppositions of a world-view presented by some within politics and the media and rises to their true height we will need to pray for revival no longer. It will have arrived and we will have dispensed with the grasshopper mentality that is one of the most insidious curses of Christendom.

The Face of a Man

John's Gospel speaks most of the divinity of Jesus but it is Luke that paints the portrait of the Son of Man.

Most of us are well aware that church is not a place we go to but the people that we are: and that its essence, in its gathered sense, is about *koinonia* – fellowship.

Having said that, there are many of us who would be aware of a sense of tranquillity in visiting ancient sites that have been used for many centuries as places of worship. Tewkesbury Abbey is just a couple of miles from our home and I know what is like to simply wander in and wonder at the intricacies of the architecture and feel a sense of awe at its grandeur. Yet as good as existential 'feel' is – that's not church and we know it's not church.

The eagle represents who we are to God in vertical spirituality and the face of man delineates who God requires us to be on a horizontal plane.

The human face of the Church towards society

Those of us who call ourselves evangelicals know that our image in the media is less than ideal. There are two reasons for this. The first has to do with the secular agenda wielded by some in the arenas of politics and media that we referred to earlier. The second emanates out of our own failure; and this area has to be the most important given that it is something over which we have a measure of control.

Secular image-profilers and spin doctors can airbrush out sad realities. The Church cannot, and should never attempt to.

The perception of evangelicals as right-wing rednecks is a caricature often cut and pasted from across the Atlantic. Sadly it is too near the truth when one watches how we portray ourselves on this side of the pond. Too often the watching world witnesses intolerant anger, venomous invective and stabbing fingers when it should be seeing something that reflects grace, mercy, open arms and a willingness to listen and engage.

Of course, there are times when lines have to be drawn in the sand, stands taken and ungodliness opposed but we are not always the best at reflecting the nature of Jesus when confronted with those things that we feel should be righteously addressed.

There remain, of course, godly leaders around the world who are endeavouring to engage in dialogue rather than in self-indulgent posturing diatribes.

Sadly, we are all too aware that it takes much less effort to shout over a wall than find a way through it. This does not mean compromising our position and selling out. It is about visiting another person's territory, listening to them and inviting them onto our ground having earned the right to be heard.

I can think of occasions when I have not always excelled in this area and when that has occurred it has risen either out of my insecurities or the weakness of my argument. The fact that you are reading this may indicate that you also consider yourself to be on a similar journey. You have not arrived, but are in the process of growing closer to where you feel God wants you to be.

Another area where Christians are blurring the battle lines and dismantling the evangelical ghetto is through our heart to serve the community. Not serving it to secure scalps and notch up numbers, but serving it because their nature is to serve. Such people realise that when Jesus fed the five thousand, he did not do it to conjure up a miracle and create a sensation. He did it because he had encountered hungry people who needed food. That is what signs and wonders are for. They are

not gifts to the Church to show off how spiritually superior we are – they are there to manifest a special sense of
God's compassion and his care. Pentecost is not a toy to
enjoy, it is a tool to use.

The human face towards those with whom we cannot entirely agree

Bigger People refuse to completely denigrate, disparage
and rubbish a brother or sister simply because they deviate from a revelation of truth that they themselves hold
dear. Bigger People do not consider themselves to hold
the final franchise on a repository of revelation upon
which they have an epistemological monopoly.

When in the company of a fellow leader I brought
up the name of a mutual acquaintance that I was
aware did not hold the precise doctrinal position of the
person I was speaking to. I had hardly got the name of
the person out of my mouth when I was interrupted
with the words, 'Oh, don't talk to me about him!' It
immediately occurred to me that the use of the phrase
'him' meant the man's whole persona – being less than
doctrinally kosher in one area now rendered him
infected in every part of his nature which seemed extended in the mind of the speaker from everything
from his scriptural exegesis to, presumably, his choice
of socks.

The human face to one another revealed through vulnerability

There is a right and wrong vulnerability. The ultimate
picture of wrong spiritual vulnerability is a life unpro-
tected by the armour of God that Paul described to the
church in Ephesus.

There are a multitude of issues that we cannot do without the assistance of God but there are also other things that we are specifically commanded to do for ourselves. The most important of these is the recognition that we are vulnerable and, that understood, to go on to embrace a willingness to protect ourselves by applying those principles that render us secure and safe from the attacks that inevitably will be launched in our direction.

Though this is true for every Christian, leaders especially should be aware of the power of shields of faith, swords of the spirit, breastplates of righteousness and belts of truth.

In the theatres of wars that have been fought on battlefields for millennia, soldiers were taught to target two types of warriors: the officers and the standard bearers. Slay a foot soldier and you have decreased the army by only a single digit. Mortally wound a high-ranking officer and you will have gone a long way to demoralise all those who have seen him fall and have looked to him for leadership in the past.

The horseman who bears aloft the regimental colours is another prime objective of the enemy. This soldier may not posses high rank but what he carries is certainly of significance. Many a weary swordsman has been reinvigorated by the sight of a regimental banner furled high and flowing in the wind. The issue is not about the value of the flag or the design of the heraldry. What matters is that the symbols conjure up stories of victory and accounts of valour – in another context we might refer to it as the essence of the vision and values of the fighting team.

The anointing that a spiritual leader 'carries' is of far more significance than the sum of his gifts or her ability to communicate. When such a leader 'falls' it is as dispiriting to Christians as a soldier that sees the company colours trampled in the mud.

If I go for a walk and lose my way I am the only one affected. If I am out for a walk with my family and become lost I have affected others. The leader, responsible for many, who strays from the path can by their actions have a catastrophic effect upon a multitude of people.

Shortly before writing this, a major figure in the evangelical world in the United States was compromised by revelations of his moral failure. The story found its way on to the British prime-news. His attainments had previously captured the attention of millions and now his demise was similarly being trumpeted internationally. Having a big ministry and a big profile does not guarantee that we are living on a large spiritual plane. The Big People that God is looking for need to be as big in the secret place where their true character resides as they are in the public square where their reputation looms large. As someone once said, character is who we are in the dark.

Some years ago when I was acting as Regional Superintendent for my denomination one of the pastors under my charge succumbed to grave moral failure.

I wrote to every minister and asked them to meet me at a central venue. In the letter I said that none were too young, too old or too spiritual to attend. As a result every minister in the country came. As folk gathered, there was no sense of people wanting to 'know the details'. Though this occurred many years ago, I still remember the sense of pride I had of the men who had assembled. Two things happened that day. The first was that we prayed for our colleague, his family and his church. Most of the time, however, was spent at looking at our own lives and doing an audit on our own personal security while recognising the importance of creating and abiding by boundaries. Big People have to be big enough to recognise their potential weakness. It is true that the higher a leader climbs the harder they fall.

There is nothing spectacular about cliff-top fences. What grabs the headlines are emergency sirens and flashing lights. Yet a fence at the top of a cliff is far better than an ambulance at the bottom.

There is a powerful passage in the Psalms of which everyone who holds a leadership position, or aspires to it, should be aware. It holds true for everyone, leader or not, who lives in a society that is quick to scream 'hypocrite' faster than a football crowd can cry 'foul'.

'May those who hope in you not be disgraced because of me, O Lord, the LORD Almighty; may those who seek you not be put to shame because of me.'[10]

Christians who fall morally will often admit, subsequent to confessing or their failure having been brought to light, that they had been in a twilight world of denial during the affair. Statements like, 'How could I have even thought of allowing myself to get into such a situation?' and 'What was I thinking of?' would not be uncommon.

Reputations built over a long period can come crashing down in an instant. It was Winston Churchill who once commented, 'To build may have to be the slow and laborious task of years. To destroy can be the thoughtless act of a single day.'

The deepest pitfall in this area is what I would term 'exceptionalism'. It manifests itself in two ways.

One guise we have already considered arises at the point we deem ourselves so spiritual we are above temptation. Another is when a believer perceives his or her personal resolve as being strong enough to resist moral danger. It is to that group that Paul writes in

Corinth when he says, 'Therefore let anyone who thinks he stands [who feels sure that he has a steadfast mind and is standing firm], take heed lest he fall [into sin].'[11]

Nor, when such failure occurs, can the Christian deflect responsibility with statements such as, 'Well, I'm only human.'

That is possibly a plausible argument prior to the New Birth but not subsequently. Continuing on theme the Apostle continues:

> For no temptation (no trial regarded as enticing to sin), [no matter how it comes or where it leads] has over-taken you and laid hold on you that is not common to man [that is, no temptation or trial has come to you that is beyond human resistance and that is not adjusted and adapted and belonging to human experience, and such as man can bear]. But God is faithful [to His Word and to His compassionate nature], and He [can be trusted] not to let you be tempted and tried and assayed beyond your ability and strength of resistance and power to endure, but with the temptation He will [always] also provide the way out (the means of escape to a landing place), that you may be capable and strong and power-ful to bear up under it patiently.

When temptation comes, God always provides the ability to overcome it. There is always a fire escape to hand – whether we are willing to use it or not.

The second expression of exceptionalism is seen in a little-known account in the life of Moses – a passage hardly ever preached upon for two reasons. The first because of the delicacy of the subject matter, the second because of a number of difficult issues arising out of the text. As this is the case it is therefore necessary to exam-ine the passage in full:

The LORD said to Moses, "When you return to Egypt, see that you perform before Pharaoh all the wonders I have given you the power to do. But I will harden his heart so that he will not let the people go. Then say to Pharaoh, 'This is what the LORD says: Israel is my firstborn son, and I told you, "Let my son go, so that he may worship me." But you refused to let him go; so I will kill your firstborn son.'" At a lodging place on the way, the LORD met [Moses] and was about to kill him. But Zipporah took a flint knife, cut off her son's foreskin and touched [Moses'] feet with it. "Surely you are a bridegroom of blood to me," she said. So the LORD let him alone. (At that time she said "bridegroom of blood", referring to circumcision.)[12]

I think that most of us would admit that if we decided to start a new religion tomorrow and wanted to create a symbol of commitment circumcision would possibly not be the first thing that would spring to mind!

God's ways, however, remain higher than ours. He was sending a powerful message that if you want what you create to grow into maturity with health and wholeness, the organ of reproduction must be healthy.

We should not be surprised therefore that churches formed out of splits and power struggles fail to grow. The organ of reproduction was not clean and what was eventually brought to life inherited a severe genetic fault. A vital chromosome was missing. The Bible calls it integrity.

God was consecrating a whole nation to himself and it was clear that whatever male was not circumcised on the eighth day was to be 'cut off'. This included Moses. Moses, or perhaps Zipporah because of an understandable reluctance to mutilate her child (this is how she would have viewed it) initially refused to comply.

There are few more powerful pictures of leadership accountability in the Scriptures than this story. We need to take a step back to see why.

Imagine that you have received a prophecy that you would one day stand before world leaders and, when that occurs, would be following the encounter up with a few breath-taking miracles.

Moses did not receive this word through a prophet – as the passage reveals the command came direct from God himself.

One might almost sympathise with Moses' supposition that, having had this promise only a short time earlier, God was more than likely to bend the rules for him given that he was apparently called to be a catalyst on an international stage.

The message from God to Moses, however, was simply, 'No, I am not going to bend the rules for you' and the message to the rest of us, leader or church member, remains the same. God does not make exceptions whoever we are, however long we have been a Christian, whatever position we hold or however scintillating our spiritual profile might appear on the outside.

With this in mind, the most important question then becomes, 'What are those fences that I need to put in place around my life?' This brings us back to the issue of vulnerability.

Continuing on the thread of little-known stories, there is an account in the book of Judges that recounts the destruction of a town called Laish[13] that is referred to as 'A peaceful and unsuspecting people'. Its naivety arose out of the fact that it remained blissfully unaware that it was a potential target by its enemy. The verses that follow offer two other reasons why their demise was only likely to be a matter of time.

We are told firstly that they lived a long way from Sidon and had no relationship with anyone else. The assumption therefore was that if they had made themselves vulnerable to their friends they would not have become vulnerable to their enemies. Accountability to others is a pre-requisite for both spiritual and emotional security.

Sidon was an ancient Phoenician city that is also mentioned in Genesis.[14] It lay on the Mediterranean coast and dominated the coastal plane adjacent to the Lebanese mountains. It was built on a hill and extended over a string of small islands connected by bridges. If only Laish had learned the importance of connectivity they would not have fallen prey to the shadow-side of vulnerability.

All of the personal discipline decisions that I have made in my life have been put in place not because of an awareness of my spiritual strength but because of an awareness of my potential for human weakness.

While well blessed with a good network of friends, and a much wider group of acquaintances, at the point I was elected to the role of General Superintendent of the Elim churches, I considered it important to be part of a group of people who were mutually accountable to one another. For the most part this was made up of those that I had known for over thirty years – since the days I was a student. We were committed to speak the truth to one another about where we were in our lives and to support one another in prayer.

In recent years, though the former relationships still remain and are important to me, I have been associated with a much smaller group – just four in all. We meet around four times a year for quality time together. Lyndon Bowring is the chairman of CARE, David Coffey former president of the Baptist World Alliance and Jeff

Lucas who, apart from being one of the senior leaders in a fifteen thousand strong church in the States, spends a large proportion of his time as a conference speaker in the UK. The format of our time together revolves around relaxing usually over an excellent meal, enjoying one another's company and sharing where we are on our particular journey. This helps us to pray more accurately and intelligently for one another between the times that we meet. Though all of us lead very busy lives, and carry a fair measure of responsibility in our various roles, these meetings are prioritised over almost everything we do. It is far more than a meeting of friends, it is safe place in which we can be real. It is a place in which the vulnerability born out of transparency cultivates a security that is both solid and robust.

Of course there is nothing new in such arrangements. When Wesley established congregations across the country his converts were encouraged to meet in small groups for a similar purpose. Throughout church history parallel networks have worked well for those that have engaged in them.

If God is to build a Church of Bigger People, in whatever context they chose to operate, those people will need to be big enough to recognise that they are not strong enough to operate in isolation.

In the four-faced Church there has to be a face presented transparently to God and a face that is open and transparent to its fellow brothers and sisters.

The face of an Ox set with a determination to serve

I am well aware that those who are reading this book, and who have a heart to grow into the expansive destiny that God has planed for them, come from a wide spectrum of the Christian Church. Some will have recently come to Christ and others will have been committed Christians for many years. There will be those from Pentecostal and charismatic backgrounds and others from far different traditions. Some will be operating as leaders within the local Church, at various levels, and others witl not.

There are some sections of the wider Church, if one were to watch how they work, that give the impression that leadership leads and those who are not leaders serve. Now it is abundantly clear in Scripture that leaders are to be given respect for their role and to expect a degree of submission to their vision. However, it is also required of leaders that they do not 'lord it over'[15] those who are entrusted to their care. This is because biblical concepts of leadership are themselves rooted in a sense of service. It matters not whether we are speaking about leadership in a cell, youth group, worship team, pastoral role or carrying denominational responsibility – service is not a one way street. The whole Church is called to serve one another in love.[16]

A person who has become a good friend in recent years is Dr James McConnell of the Metropolitan Tabernacle in Belfast. This tremendous church, affiliated to our denomination, was founded with a handful of people by Dr McConnell when he was a young man and has grown to be one of the largest churches in Europe. It has four thousand in attendance on a Sunday and a weekly Bible study that attracts over a thousand people. Through its television ministry it reaches many millions more around the world.

I have an abiding memory of the last time I preached there. What is conjured up in my mind as I reflect on the occasion is not the multi-million pound building, the amazing music ministry or the warm-hearted and welcoming congregation. It was the journey my wife and I made on our way to the evening service.

The weather was horrendous with teeming rain lashing down against a black and menacing sky. As our driver pulled closer I saw among the many who manned the huge car park a man with an umbrella silhouetted against the yellow light that poured out of the church building. As we drew closer I saw to my amazement that the figure was none other than James McConnell himself. When we had raced from the elements to the shelter of the sanctuary I asked him what on earth he was doing. In his warm Ulster brogue he replied, 'Oh, I've spent time every Sunday doing that for years – I just want to serve.'

At the time of writing my good friend Pastor George McKim is preparing to assume leadership of this great church. My appreciation of him will not be at all diminished if he fails to continue with this custom as I know him to be a man who serves the church in a multitude of other ways. I, for my part, have never done car park duty and I have no immediate plans to pencil it in to my schedule. That is not the point. What struck me about that moment, and what will remain perpetually in my memory, is that the thousands who pass through that church receive not only a powerful message from the pulpit but a sermon about service before they ever reach the door of the building.

Big People must never be too tall to stoop. We have an apple tree in our garden and one thing that I have always noticed is that the branches with the most fruit always hang the lowest while the ones with the least fruit on their branches are the most exalted – they remain lofty but empty.

Yet this third face, if it confines its gaze to the Church alone, still fails to be a full manifestation of the nature of Christ. Jesus announces his purpose not simply as coming to serve the Church but to 'seek and to save those that are lost'.[17]

To reflect Christ well means to serve not only those we know, and love those who love us, but to serve a world that has not yet encountered Christ and may even have its face set against him.

There have been remarkable inter-denominational expressions of doing this effectively, throughout the UK in recent years. 'Soul in the City' sends hundred of young people into an area – not to shout Scripture texts into startled faces like tossing a hand grenade into a crowd – but to clean up graffiti-scarred walls, remove litter and cut grass among a multitude of other serving roles.

The work of Andy Hawthorne in Manchester with the Eden project is yet another example of the Church's commitment to its community. Its evangelists do not blow in, blow up and blow out – they choose to set up home in areas known as 'sink estates' around the city. In the past, Christians have seen it as an expression of the favour of God to get out of such areas. Now they see it as part of the heart of God to get into them.

This vision has been replicated in a multitude of similar, though smaller, scenarios throughout the nation. For the most part, they have been birthed out of the local church. It is the arena in which unsung heroes play their part and unnamed prophets declare a message that is bigger than themselves. They preach a gospel that they portray in lifestyle and which touches the whole person. They have become the message that they purport to proclaim.

This does not mean that the gospel need not be preached in the traditional sense of the word. Neither is there any doubt that Christians need to immerse themselves in the teaching of the Bible to the point that they can to coherently explain its message.

Bigger People serve others through affirmation, the respecting of potential and the declaration that God has far more for them than they are currently experiencing.

While I was writing this chapter I fulfilled a ministry appointment in Portadown, Northern Ireland. On the way from the airport to my hotel, Edwin Michael senior pastor of the six hundred-strong congregation, asked me if I wanted to visit their drop-in centre at the heart of the town. He told me that it was staffed by both full-time workers and volunteers and catered for troubled teenagers who had engaged in drugs, glue sniffing, alcohol and other addictive lifestyles. The person who conducted me around the facility, and who was one of the full-time staff, I was later to learn had links with terrorism prior to becoming a Christian. I was eager to see what was happening but was about to be surprised by what I saw. I had anticipated that though it was likely to be larger in scale, it would be similar to scores of other inner-city ventures I had seen before that were intended to 'give the kids something to do and keep them out of trouble'.

What I was not expecting was a 'wow factor'. As I entered the complex I immediately noticed that everything was state-of-the-art from the IT section, the big-screen computer gaming room and refreshment area. What made this place different was that there was an absence of cast-off furniture, old settees or threadbare carpets. The immaculate black leather sofas reminded me more of the lobby of a corporate headquarters. The obvious question was, 'Why so much investment at such a high level?' but the more crucial one was 'How is it that this stuff has not been slashed and the place trashed?'

I was told that the very same teenagers who were sitting around nearby had wrecked places similar to this in the past. The difference was that the members of this Portadown church did not see them as 'trouble to be controlled' but people of worth to God and to whom should therefore be given the best. They were serving the kids not with charity but with something far greater – affirmation. Married to this approach was a zero-tolerance culture in the centre. Yet even this created a framework of discipline that said, 'We respect you enough to believe that you are capable of respecting those around you and the environment that has been provided for you.'

Seven thousand miles away in Huntington Park California a staggering example of service through affirmation was birthed in the early eighties which has been the result of tens of thousands of people around the world finding Christ.

I first heard of the 'Praise Chapel' network of churches subsequent to one of their leaders passing on a book of mine to their founder which resulted in me being invited to speak at a conference of theirs in California.

In the eighties, a young pastor and his wife leading a congregation of around sixty people began seeing people come to Christ whose background had been in extortion, violence and mafia-related crime.

The response of most ministers, and possibly myself, would have been to see these people move through a process of discipleship and, as time passed, integrate themselves as regular members of the church.

Mike and Donna Neville heard God tell them something far more radical. They concluded that if the man who was the writer of a large proportion of the New Testament could describe himself as the 'chief of sinners' responsible for the torture and death of others – why could not these new converts also become apostolic leaders and church planters?

A revival broke out. Hundreds of people gave their life to Christ in the Los Angeles area and went on to plant

churches across the USA. The network then mushroomed
from one continent to another – for the most part led by
people who had previously been figures in the world of
violence, extortion and drugs.

On my first visit to preach to this group I asked one
man who was now a senior leader with Praise Chapel
what his background had been. He explained that he
had not lived a violent lifestyle but had been the principal figure in a money-laundering operation throughout
America. I asked if any in his congregation, numbering
several hundred, had been indicted for murder. He told
me over thirty had served time for that crime and were
now serving the Lord. Another man who had been a
notorious embezzler was, unbelievably, the financial
administrator for a group of the churches and was particularly known now for his fiscal integrity.

During the nineties, Mike Neville died following a
short illness. The whole denomination, now with hundreds of churches straddling the globe, asked his widow,
Donna, to give leadership to the organisation. This was
remarkable on many levels, not least because the majority of those in the organisation came from a Hispanic
culture where women leadership was far from the norm.
But Mike and Donna Neville had sown greatness in
them, had shown affirmation, and discipled them into
bigger people than they could ever have imagined being
possible. The group that began with a handful of people
in a small church and now numbering many thousands
proved to be even bigger in spirit than their culture and
overwhelmingly affirmed her as their leader.

Donna Neville, who has spoken as principal speaker
at the Elim Conference, is one of the most outstanding
Bible teachers I have heard. She continues to lead her
own church in the Los Angeles area and the overall
international vision for the Praise Chapel churches is led

by Mike's brother. Larry and Janet Neville are two out-standing people. Their theme is 'connectivity'. They believe that affirming grace in the life of individuals, whatever their background, and ensuring they connect with the culture is the precursor to evangelistic effec-tiveness.

In 2006 Jack Hayford and I were among the speakers at the World Conference of this group in Phoenix, Arizona. Their heart for church planting is infectious. Their zeal to go to the most difficult parts of the world trusting God for their safety and support springs out of the biblical principle, 'He, or she, who has been forgiven much – loves much'.[18]

There is a huge spiritual power behind affirmation and encouragement. Too often the Church uses guilt as a motivating tool. If it works at all it does so only in the short term. Condemnation can get you off the starting block but it can never grant you the stamina in your spirit that will spur you on to complete the race.

Consider someone climbing a hill while pushing a boulder in front of them. The gradient is steep and the climber has not only slowed to a standstill but is now wondering if the heavy stone might soon roll back on him. Momentum has totally stalled. There are only a few options.

The first might be to condemn the climber for their lack of progress while, at the same time, pointing out to them that there are others you know who could push a heavier boulder twice as fast. Some might even regale the weary person with stories of their youth when they accomplished similar feats of endurance with the mini-mum of effort. The sad fact is that, even if these accounts were true, the stone is not moved a millimetre further. On the contrary, the struggler is likely to become as weak in spirit as she is in physical strength.

If instead the strategy were to be changed to pointing out footholds, offering nourishment and applying a shoulder to the stone – progress might begin to be made.

It strikes me that there is a colossal need within the home, the workplace and the church for a Christian culture of affirmation.

Most people associate the Day of Pentecost with the moment in history when people first spoke in tongues yet there was something far more important than that taking place. The clothing of power that came upon the 120 people gathered was the commencement of a revolution that would later turn the world upside down and was, and remains, the primary purpose of Pentecost.

Accompanying this outpouring was a sometimes forgotten phenomenon: the tongues of fire that rested on everyone's head. Imagine for a moment that you had been present at that powerful prayer meeting. Consider what it might have been like to become aware of this manifestation on the head of your friend. Momentarily you may conclude that they are experiencing something of which you had been denied. The reality was that everyone was experiencing the same miracle though, understandably, none could see the fire on their own head.

Affirming 'someone else's fire' can be hugely supportive to them and the encouragement applied is likely to accelerate them on to believe God for even greater things in the future.

It was the practice in one of the churches that I pastored that in the Monday evening cell groups the congregation discuss how to put into practice the things God had been saying to the church the previous day. I used to visit each of the groups in turn and, on the occasion I am about to recount, the subject I had been preaching on just twenty-four hours earlier was, 'How to discover the gift of God in your life.' The problem was that discussion soon stalled because of an innate British reticence to identify publicly any perceived gift that one may have.

The cell-group leader quickly solved the impasse by suggesting that the group shared what they saw God doing in the lives of the other members. It was a moving moment – a powerful time as each described the fire they saw on each other's head.

Bigger People are born out of a culture of encouragement and very soon become encouragers themselves. It is the very DNA of growth and progress. It is the neglected side of service; for it is sometimes easier to *do* something for someone than to put something into someone that will spur them on to enhance their own personal achievement. The former serves our spirit and makes us feel useful. The latter serves their destiny and causes them to fulfil the purpose for which they have been called of God.

The face of the ox reminds us that the posture of our life, in its entirety, creates a presence through which our message is understood. The tongue is not the only tool by which truth is told. The servant's towel is a powerful instrument by which the gospel is articulated.

The face of the lion set with a determination to endure and to conquer

If you have ever felt that life wasn't fair, you were right.

It isn't fair that a quarter of the world's population live on less than £2 per week. It isn't fair that one third of the world are without electricity and that four billion of the planet's population have access to neither cash nor credit.

The fully rounded message of the gospel proclaims the need for equity and social justice now. Though salvation means that we have passed from the kingdom of darkness to the kingdom of light, and God's invisible kingdom is in the hearts of his subjects, this does not preclude the need to invest our energies in creating societal change. Jesus spoke of letting our light shine in the darkness of our current culture so that people seeing our good works might glorify our father.[19]

It is Matthew's Gospel that speaks most of Jesus as being king. The Sermon on the Mount is the manifesto and the parables of the kingdom permeate the entire biblical account.

The invisible kingdom will one day be followed by a visible kingdom – in which Christ will reign and through which the Old Testament prophecy will be fulfilled as the 'knowledge of the glory of the Lord covers the Earth as the waters cover the sea'.[20]

It is vital however that the Church does not drift into long sightedness centred on a future hope and consequently ignores the present plight of those suffering.

The eschatology taught in many denominations speaks of an end-time period called the Great Tribulation. The Left Behind series of novels that have sold throughout the Christian world in multiple millions talk of a terrible period in which the anti-Christ will cause unprecedented persecution in the years preceding the return of Christ to rule the Earth.

While I firmly believe in the personal return of Christ and also believe in a tribulation period, I have to say that the factional nature of Christian literature (the mingling of fact and fiction) often only serves to draw attention away from the millions who have already been martyred for their faith and especially the countless thousands who are currently suffering and dying today simply because they refuse to recant their faith in Christ.

As you read these pages, parents in the Sudan have their babies torn from them and sold for the equivalent of pence in the market place. If they ever reach adolescence they will be sold as slaves to Islamic owners. As this chapter was being written the world news records the death sentence placed upon those in Pakistan who have converted to Christ and who now will die for their faith. Millions of Christian believers perished, many through starvation and torture under Communism. What Christians in North Korea are enduring right now cannot be transmitted to the printed page as the accounts are too harrowing to be included here. One thing is sure – nothing in a Great Tribulation could be any worse than what countless thousands of our brothers and sisters are going through as the clock ticks around at this very moment.

What is particularly unfair is that, while we in the west enjoy freedom to worship and own a Bible, every year one hundred and sixty thousand men and women around the world are martyred simply for following Jesus.

Yes, you read that correctly, that number does not represent those who are persecuted and harassed (that toll would be in the millions) these are those who have be slaughtered because they will not renounce the faith that you and I enjoy and sometimes take for granted.

Figures recently released have revealed that, if persecution of the church gets no worse, one Christian in every two hundred people alive today can expect to die for their faith. Currently the probability is that this horrific toll will be exacted in parts of the world other than our own.

One of the most challenging texts to practice is, 'Remember those in prison as if you were their fellow-prisoners, and those who are ill-treated as if you yourselves were suffering.'[21]

When we pray we must not simply see them as powerless *victims* of Islamic or Communist oppression. These heroic men, women and young people have consciously chosen to follow Christ, whatever the cost to themselves.

As you read these lines, Christians in seventy-eight countries are undergoing persecution. Again, their only crime is that they have chosen to follow Christ.

When I return to the west from places that I have ministered in for only a short time I vow I will never again complain about the minutiae that frays the average westerner's nerves – westerners who have plenty of money and freedom – and do not live in a country savaged by persecution. The tragedy is, and I may not be alone in this, that within weeks I find myself, once more, all too easily agitated about my failure to secure a parking space in a the car park of a shopping centre where, if I never bought a luxury item again I would live richer than do millions around the world.

The argument here is not to induce guilt. Writers, preachers and the rest of us can so easily fall into the trap of believing that because we have highlighted need we have somehow met it. We have done nothing until we have done something.

I do not want to embrace the kind of persecution that others are facing, but there is no doubt that the Church is always refined, pruned and made stronger when it occurs. The presence of eighty million believers in China bears witness to that. There is much evidence that the current political regime is slowly allowing unprecedented freedom – and this is running in parallel with the burgeoning economy. I have met Chinese Christians who have said, and I do not know whether they are right or wrong in this, that the church in China could be weakened by the relaxation of such constraints rather than strengthened. Time will tell.

On a trip to Eastern Europe I engaged in conversation with a fellow passenger during the flight. She had been brought up as a teenager under a harsh communist dictatorship. She told me that, while she had no wish to return to the past, not all the changes had been good ones. She spoke of a new capitalism that had nurtured selfishness and weakened community. Others I have spoken with relate a similar mantra: that political freedom does not necessarily engender a freedom to do that which is right.

The dark hand of persecution rises and falls with its shadow over different continents and in different periods of history and, in its wake, brings persecution in different and increasingly insidious forms.

It is my belief that, in the UK, the persecution of the Church will be fiscal before it is physical. A secularising agenda would prefer to throw faith-based institutions into debt before throwing them into jail. It is not the looming spectre of the prison system but the insidious use of the tax system about which we should be most concerned.

By changing tax laws governments succeed in undermining the institution of marriage by making it more financially advantageous for people not commit to a lifelong covenant together.

Roman Catholic adoption agencies are currently being threatened with closure unless they adopt the government's code of ethics rather than one that is based on biblical principles. Secularist evangelists preach with religious zeal about a tolerant society but their tolerance tends to evaporate where Christianity is concerned.

At a family function I chatted with a fellow guest who was both a politician and a professing Christian. He told me that only a few years ago his view on homosexuality was understood. It appeared to be accepted that, as a

Christian, he could hold a view different to those who believed that homosexuality was an acceptable lifestyle. Today due to the power of our 'politically correct' media, he is not allowed to state his point of view in public. On the contrary, it is demanded of him that he endorse such a lifestyle under threat of loosing his seat and his career. The reality is that his position as a politician in this account is incidental – today he could have been a member of almost any profession and risk losing his job on account of his Christian stand.

It is my view that the next stage will be to control not only what the individual believes but what the Church teaches.

Most church buildings are zero-rated for rates. Many of them are in city centres occupying prime locations in their area. Were the zero-rating to be removed, they could have a financial burden that would make their presence in their premises financially unsustainable.

There is also a move to have tax relief on charity giving constrained. Some secular fundamentalists have realised that this would not only suspend building expansion but would put some churches in a position where they could no longer afford to pay a minister.

If the criteria for tax relief and zero-rating is related to the message that politicians allow the church to proclaim, serious choices will have to be made.

I have no doubt at all that should that day come, and there are many indications that it will, the Church will not only survive but will be galvanised further into action. It is unstoppable and it will prevail.

The face of the eagle will be raised to pray, the face of man will be raised in integrity, the face of the ox will be raised by a church that will serve its community whatever the constraints and the face of the lion will be raised with a roar that proclaims not only its willingness to endure but to overcome.

Jesus promised that he would build his church and that the gates of hell would not overcome it.[22]

3

A Bigger Voice

Bigger does not necessarily mean louder and most certainly does not mean strident. The world is not waiting for a voice that bellows truth at them but that articulates cogently and coherently a message that is perceived by them to parallel with a life experience that they understand. People usually recoil from noise but are drawn to the eloquence of relevance.

In a church I once pastored a lady spoke to me about the frustration she was feeling as her husband had not come to faith. 'I have done everything I could possibly do and prayed until I am weary with prayer,' she complained.

When I asked about how she had been conducting herself I was told that she raised the subject of Christian things with her husband at every conceivable opportunity. No TV report, news item or matter of conversation was too trivial that she could not add some spiritual significance to it. Packing his case on a business trip she had included worthy Christian paperbacks with spectacular testimonies. She went on to say that recently when he woke in the morning a open Bible had been strategically placed on his bedside table so that his first awareness on stirring from sleep would be the need to be saved. What more could she do? I suggested that she started by not shouting with her words and instead seek to be the best wife to him that she could be.

When we lived in Scotland two of our neighbours asked us to explain what it meant to be a Christian. When the conversation ended I expressed to my wife that I felt that the husband, who had shown the most interest, was very close to committing his life to the Lord. However, a few days later it was his wife that took the step rather than him. We were delighted that Margaret had come to faith but surprised that David had not been the first to respond to God.

A few weeks later as I phoned home from an engagement abroad my wife told me that David wanted to see me as soon as possible on my return. Both of us felt we knew what the urgency was and why he wanted to see me. We were right. David wanted to commit his life to Christ.

After I had prayed with him I enquired why he had taken so long to come to a decision. He told me that though he had felt drawn to respond straight away, he felt that the process of commitment to Christ appeared too easy. He found it strange that something so vital and life-changing could be so simple. He resolved to allow Margaret to take the step first and then to see what happened. He said that they had a great marriage and were very much in love. He had absolutely no complaints about their relationship. However, in the weeks that had followed he had seen a transformation in her that left him wanting what she had, and experiencing for himself what she had discovered.

Two Christian voices: two entirely different results.

The Voice of the Primary Passion

Although the Church, to be effective, needs to display all of its faces to effectively portray Christ to the world, local congregations often have their own emphases that reflect an identity of particular importance to them. We could refer to this as a primary passion. This of itself is not wrong of course and is to be commended.

A church in an inner city with a heart for the poor is going to operate differently to a congregation in an affluent village in a stockbroker belt (though of course the biblical use of the word 'poor' remains more expansive than the fiscal connotation that we tend to attach to it).

The problem only arises when a group becomes locked into an ideology that interprets everything it sees in the light of its own primary passion and subsequently cannot recognise any manifestation of ministry other than its own.

If a photographer looks at a landscape with a naked eye she will get a true representation of the scene before her. This will also occur if she views the same scene through a lens. If, however, she threads in a red filter her whole world becomes red – fields, skies, lakes and even snow. From that point, everything captured takes on a similar hue. Something has been interposed between the camera and reality and has subsequently distorted the true picture.

When I turn on certain Christian TV channels and catch a prosperity preacher in full flight it appears that every verse in the Bible is honed to present a picture of enhanced financial blessing. Most of us have no problem in believing that God wants to bless his people – the difficulty comes when a passion acts as a filter that tends to taint an entire world-view.

Some groups have had a filter attached to them by others – their names having sprung from a doctrinal emphasis that they had sought to restore to the church in their formative years. No one really believes that Presbyterians have little interest in anything outside of church government, that Baptists are solely focussed on total immersion or that Pentecostals spend all their time speaking in tongues.

As vision can be blurred by inaccurate interpretation so the voice of the Church can be distorted by the static interference of misplaced emphasis.

The Voice of the Ventriloquist

There are Christian movements that span the globe which were conceived at the point their founders experienced a wholly legitimate encounter with God and, as a result, have been major catalysts that have rightly challenged established thinking about the need for the Church to change.

When the doors of Wittenberg Cathedral reverberated to the noise of nails being hammered into it as an obscure monk called Martin Luther attached his list of 95 stinging rebukes to Pope Leo X, it was the thunder that preceded a theological storm across the world. By the time he died in 1543 the spiritual landscape of Europe had irreversibly altered.

Courageous encounters that lead to persecution and martyrdom have, in other contexts, proved to be the precursors to new movements and sometimes national awakenings.

Such interventions are vital if the Church is to continually evolve and take the shape that the Holy Spirit has designed it to be. Revelation, however, should always be a primary voice and never a secondary echo.

There is a danger that the local church, reacting out of frustration to seeing little spiritual fruit, reads about success in another part of the world and then immediately endeavours to replicate it in their context. When this occurs the results are often disastrous.

That is not to say that lessons cannot be learned or some principles effectively applied. The difficulty arises when it is assumed that vision can be imported as a 'job lot' as if it were little more than a consignment of cocoa or bale of hay.

The issue is not about whether someone else's vision is valid. The vision may be entirely valid for them. It is just that it is rarely portable or transferable in its original form.

I write this book on a computer running Windows XP. I am informed that a newer operating system, Vista, has features my current configuration does not possess. I am prepared to believe it but I am also prepared to believe that to indiscriminately import Vista features to my current computer may result not only in them not working but the creation of a danger that what I already have in place, and has worked well until now, could be completely corrupted. The issue is not about whether Vista is good, it is about portability.

Churches have been split, and their spiritual operating systems corrupted, because its leaders and people alike have failed to realise that you can't successfully clone revelation.

What brought spiritual renewal in one context has often been the result of a long journey and perhaps protracted pain. That preparatory period of incubation cannot be faxed into a new framework without serious consequences. Vision can come via the lightening strike of Damascus road experiences but it is more often born out of process. It cannot be lifted out of a paperback book, DVD or seminar notes and be expected to slot into place in an instant.

The possibilities of potential problems are exacerbated when new vision is brought in by a prophetic word that has been neither weighed nor assessed.

As the leader of a Pentecostal Movement it will comes as no surprise that I believe in spiritual gifts. However, the very fact that the Bible requires us to test prophecy reveals to us that revelatory words have a potential to be contaminated. Prophecy can become polluted. The most toxic additives are the human spirit and a personal agenda. We must not despise prophesying but we must not listen to it with spiritual naivety.

I, possibly like many who are reading this chapter, keep a spiritual journal. I do not use it as a diary or always add to it daily, but I would be sure to record moments that I believe are significant for me – lessons I am learning or revelations I feel that I have received. A few of those encounters would have taken the form of a 'word' that someone has felt the inclination to share with me through an initiative that they feel has begun with God. I am grateful for those who have done this and there are times when I have found such intimations pivotal in my life.

There are those, however, who place personal words almost on a par with Scripture and appear to see them as an addendum to their Bible. They take the form of a personal 'Revelation Chapter 23'.

They would argue that if the Scriptures are God-breathed and the prophecy to them inspired by the Holy Spirit, then why should they not be held on a par. There are several reasons but one of them would be that while scriptural principles are timeless; personal words are often pertinent to a period, a single window in time, of a person's life.

Vision, especially where the vision is used to shape the nature of Church, is only valid at the point that it comes from a place of personal encounter. Echoes are not sustainable and by their nature fade and evaporate like the tail of a comet diminishing as it goes. Only authentic revelation carries with it the genetic code that guarantees growth, longevity, durability and health.

What appears to be an almost off-hand statement by Elisha[1] in the account of the widow and the oil, turns out to be the very key to the miracle.

Much is made of the fact that she was told by the prophet to collect as many vessels as she could. Little weight is given to the fact that she was instructed to ensure that the vessels were empty. The widow concerned was a good woman whose husband, now dead, was being faced with a crippling burden of debt so heavy that she was at the point of losing her sons to slavery as part payment of her obligations.

Imagine for a moment that the woman comes to your doorstep and asks for a vessel. The first thing you are likely to do is to ask her why she wants the container. In this way you will determine size and shape. When she tells you it should be able to hold oil, I have little doubt what your next response is likely to be.

You live with her in the same small rural community and will be aware of the tragedies that have struck her family. You will know her as the wife of a prophet and have possibly been helped by her or her husband in the past. Neither will the fact that she is in danger of losing her sons be lost on you.

Your reflex reaction I am sure is to come to her aid with more than a pot but with a contribution of your own oil – either as a gift or a loan.

For her part the temptation is a very real one. She knows that if she visits two hundred homes and gets two hundred gifts of oil her short-term needs will be met. The problem is that she will increase her income for a while, but the new injection of supply will stop far short of the miracle she needs.

How does this account parallel with the reflected voice and the cloned revelation?

When the minister preaches to the congregation, he will have spent considerable time in prayer and preparation beforehand. As you are blessed and fed you are in fact receiving an overflow of his oil. When the Worship Team minister, and you are brought into an increased sense of the presence of God, you are getting an overflow from their oil as they will have waited on God long before the service began The same is true of watching Christian media or even reading a book of this nature.

Clearly all of these ways of blessing and input are right, legitimate and good. The problem is that it is possible to survive your entire Christian life on the overflow of other people's oil.

The problem is also compounded in that the widow does not yet know for certain that divine intervention is on the way: and why should she refuse to take something that is tangible now rather than a miracle that may not materialise?

Her choice is between total provision and top-up provision.

If these things are part of God's ministry to us then what is the problem? There is no problem at all. It's simply that sometimes the good is the enemy of the best.

How about saying to God:

> Thank you for my leaders, my church and the many forms of Christian media that minister to me. But today Lord, I am coming to you totally empty. I want you to bless me for me – not just because you have blessed someone else who is being a blessing to me. I want to wait on you until, out of the time I spend in your presence, I reach a place of personal fullness. I want to stay here until, out of a place of dryness, I experience refreshing. I am going

to remain until I discover your purpose and plan for my life. I will not despise these other vital means that you have placed at my disposal but, from today, my core choice is not for third-party dependence on blessing. I will dig my own well and from that place receive the supply that will consistently nourish my soul.

Elijah knew that gestures from the village, however well intentioned, would actually prove a hindrance to the woman rather than a help. He knew that the widow, like the rest of us, needed to come empty before God for miraculous provision to occur (in whatever form it may take).

We will examine other principles that arise from this miracle in a later chapter.

The Voice of Perceived Hostility

Leadership magazine interviewed a group of senior pastors who led mega-churches in the United States and asked them about how they dealt with sermon preparation. Several spoke of time spent in prayer and others about hours of research and biblical study that went into each and every message. When they were asked what was the last thing that they did prior to the presentation of the message, most referred to praying for the sermon to be effectively received by the hearers. Only one preacher differed.

He said that the last thing that he did was to sit in his study with his notes in front of him. He would then imagine a representative group of people from his church looking at him from the other side of the desk. One might be a successful businessman, another an unemployed person existing on benefit, another an elderly person living alone and yet another, a young person struggling with adolescent angst. Having scrutinized the faces of each person he then scanned his completed notes to see if there was relevance that would touch each of their life experiences. If he found that his sermon notes did not pass such a litmus test, they were adjusted accordingly.

What he was saying was that the effectiveness of his delivery depended not just on the source of inspiration and the truth of the word, but by the contexts into which his message would be delivered. I consider this sound advice to all who preach or teach.

What unfortunately sometimes happens is that the message becomes manipulated by the hearers to such a degree that a small minority of people, sometimes even a single individual, has the potential power to hijack the pulpit from the place they sit in the pew.

I am well aware that those reading this will be both leaders and members of the local church. What follows will be viewed from two vantage points but the lesson, if we are to be a Bigger People, has to be learned from both perspectives.

During one period of my pastoral ministry there were a small group of people who had set themselves in opposition to the vision that I, the elders and the vast majority of the congregation, felt was God's destiny for us as a church.

These good folk usually positioned themselves in the back rows of the church – their body language giving amplified articulation to their dissent. Even though in a large congregation, where the vast majority were engaged in worship and passionately behind all that God was doing, I found my attention drawn to them like a magnet every time I preached and could not help but notice as they glowered in my direction with folded arms and 'bless me if you dare' stares.

Most ministers would admit that if they heard four hundred people at the end of a message telling them how much they were blessed by it, and one person who expressed that they disagreed intensely, it is the one and not the four hundred that they would be thinking about on the journey home from church.

Those who were in dissent did not only manage to draw my attention during the service, I found myself preaching against the things they represented – which I would have described at the time as a pharisaic attitude and a religious spirit. I may well have been right in my conclusions but the effect it had on me began to distort my perspective – something that often happens when leadership is challenged.

Elijah had a Mount Carmel experience in which he defeated the prophets of Baal and called fire down from heaven: yet moments later he is found with suicidal thoughts under a juniper tree because of the opposition of just one woman.

My wife was the one who drew my attention to what was happening by suggesting that if I continued my assault on the few, the many would not get fed. She was right and my preaching eventually came back on course.

Nehemiah, when building the walls of Jerusalem, refused to fall into the trap that for a short time I had succumbed to. When he was asked to refrain from building in order to enter into dialogue with his detractors, he refused to do so.[2] He was embarked on a bigger project and Bigger People can only do big things if they make up their minds to refrain to engage with minutiae.

Periodically news stories appear about whales beached on the seashore. On one occasion, having read a story of this nature, I felt that there was something to be learned spiritually from such tragedies and, when I researched in more detail, I found that there was.

Ironically, the species most prone to the problem is the pilot whale. I learned that they become stranded for one of two reasons. One is that their leaders become disorientated and lose a sense of direction. The other is that, while chasing shoals of small fish, they inadvertently wander from the deep waters for which they were created and end up in the shallows. I am sure that the parallel needs no further unpacking from me.

The Voice of the Sponsor

When serialised radio shows commenced in the USA they were often sponsored by a single commercial enterprise that financed the whole show. Throughout the storyline, and often when the tension in the narrative was at its height, an announcer would annoyingly interrupt with a line such as, 'Will our hero survive their assailants attack? Find out after this short break. This programme is brought to you today by . . .' Many of these businesses marketed household detergents and so the phrase 'soap operas' was born. There was nothing insidious in this. It was just a good marketing opportunity.

In the 1950s everyone wanted a TV and soap operas appeared on our screens as well as on our radios. As this was a visual medium, actors began to work within sets rather than standing anonymously behind microphones.

Imagine a scene that centres around a story based in a family kitchen where the director places props to add a sense of realism. He would be certain to place a box of washing powder where the camera would easily pick it up, and it would be inconceivable that he would provide any other brand than that of the sponsor.

In Victorian times it was not uncommon for parishes in parts of England to be financed by wealthy landowners who would patronise, in the literal sense of the word, the vicar and his family. Their family pew was reserved and the last thing the minister would consider would be to preach at variance with his patron's theological position. Church practice would be unlikely to ever deviate from the position of those who held the purse strings. Though the minister may have all of his natural faculties of speech he had, to all intents and purposes, lost his voice, were external pressure ever to be applied. He had become a ventriloquist's dummy. His leadership potential was neutered and, in reality, had become little more than a puppet.

When the Scripture says that 'Fear of man will prove to be a snare,'[3] it means fear renders him immobile and unable to move.

This remains a particular danger today in small congregations where direction is dictated, not by leadership, but by controlling families who have a disproportionate influence due to their numbers. It can also occur when undue regard is given to someone of influence. Wealth or status can cause inertia to the degree that a minister is trapped like a rabbit in the headlights of a car – overwhelmed by the luminaries who the minister may perceive put him the shade.

In forty years of ministry I have pastored several congregations whose members include those who have either wealth or social status. On no occasions have any of them sought to use their power to influence disproportionately the direction of the church. On the contrary, in the vast majority of occasions such people have operated with both humility and personal integrity within the fellowship.

We would be naïve however to assume that it cannot or does not happen.

I was teaching on this subject at a leadership conference and at the close of the meeting was approached by a young minister. He told me that he had been appointed to a small congregation whose worship style was of a type popular half a century ago. The musicians had told him that any attempt by him to transition to anything more contemporary would result in them leaving the church. They knew of course that there were currently no other musicians to take their place and were effectively holding the church hostage.

Pastors and elders should act with sensitivity when seeking to change and we all know of situations where churches have been wrecked by those who have acted arrogantly and without managing change sensibly. Inordinately rapid change can be as disastrous as trying to change the tyres while a car is still in motion.

Having said that, when leadership loses its voice, leadership ceases to lead.

Bigger People move strongly and consistently, even if that sometimes means more slowly. What matters is that the goal is reached with as many people on board as possible. What must never happen is a 'Gulliver' allowing himself to be confined to inertia by 'Lilliputians' whose suffocating threads of minutiae straitjacket him into immobility.

We have considered the external pressures on the voice but the internal causes are every bit as insidious. We lose our voice spiritually for the very same reasons we lose it physically.

Infection One of the saddest scenarios in this regard that I can recall was that of a minister who in his youth was a popular speaker at conferences and Bible weeks around the country and across the denominations. He was a skilled communicator and his teaching possessed depth and insight. Unfortunately, however, through a breakdown in relationship with other leaders, he became affected by a cynicism that developed into over-whelming bitterness. He still had something to say, but because his spirit was wrong, the invitations to speak dried up. His spirit had become infected and he effec-tively lost his voice. Most throat infections are of a rela-tively short duration. Sadly, his lasted until the day he died.

Pressure and Strain Were we to ask the biblical Hannah what one word would have described her, her answer would most certainly have been 'barrenness' – the inability to conceive and bring a child into the world. It filled her every waking thought. She carried the stigma like a shroud and was engulfed in a constant sense of inadequacy and shame. Her internal pain was so great that when she entered the place of prayer Eli the priest came to the conclusion that she must be drunk, and unfairly rebuked her for it. What he had witnessed was a mouth moving without sounds com-ing from it. In her protracted pain, Hannah had lost her voice.

Her story had a happy ending and we know that she was eventually able to regain her joy: but the process was painful and no one should underestimate the power of frustration, and lack of growth, for their ability to steal our song.

The lament of God's people in captivity is recorded in the psalms:

> By the rivers of Babylon we sat and wept when we remembered Zion. There on the poplars we hung our harps . . . How can we sing the songs of the LORD while in a foreign land? If I forget you, O Jerusalem, may my right hand forget [its skill]. May my tongue cling to the roof of my mouth . . .[4]

Tiredness, weariness, pressure and strain can all too easily cause us to 'hang up our harps' in despair.

Some pain is too acute to be articulated. Sometimes the most eloquent prayer God ever hears is our tears. The Scriptures says that at such times the Holy Spirit intercedes for us with 'groans that words cannot express'.[5]

This was Hannah's experience but God heard her just the same.

There are very few long prayers in the Bible. What we know as the Lord's Prayer, spans a wide gamut of petition and praise and can be uttered in around twenty seconds. The most powerful prayer that Peter ever prayed was when he considered himself at the point of drowning. The three words 'Lord save me!'[6] was all that was necessary. No evangelical jargon and worthy phrases – just an expression of desperation.

If, as you read this, you are among those who are 'lost for words' because of what you are facing – be encouraged that there is what we might call, a 'vocabulary of the valley' that does not depend on sentences, syntax or prose. It is nevertheless heard in heaven and something to which God responds.

There are two places where the voice of the Church must be heard.

Getting Heard on Earth

Of the fifty thousands sermons preached in the UK every Sunday, the sad thing is that many of the messages are little more than the personal philosophies of the speaker. Were each preacher a simple conduit by which heaven touches earth, as we recognised earlier, we would no longer need to pray for revival: it would already be with us.

The preacher is primarily a postman. It does not matter what status, years of experience or academic accolades he or she might hold – if the preacher fails to be a postman they have failed.

Consider this for a moment. All the letters delivered to our home are delivered by the postman but we never receive one that has been written by the postman himself.

Imagine an electricity bill falling open at the wrong side of the door and the postman sees that a charge has been made for £250. If he were to take a pen and strike out the final zero because he happens to like the occupants of the house let me ask you 'Would he be a good or a bad postman?' He may consider himself to be a well-intentioned friend. Sadly, however, were he to alter the invoice, he would have failed to fulfil the role for which he has been commissioned. His sole value and the reason he is employed, is to faithfully deliver a message that has been communicated by another.

Preachers have not been commissioned by God to inflict upon their hearers their personal world-view. Their function is to bring the word of God. Nor is it their place to edit or censor the missive to make it more palatable. It is not without significance that the closing words of the last chapter of the book of Revelation read

> I warn everyone who hears the words of the prophecy of this book: If anyone adds anything to them, God will add to him the plagues described in this book. And if anyone takes words away from this book of prophecy, God will take away from him his share in the tree of life and in the holy city, which are described in this book.[7]

Bigger than my box

We all rightly rejoice in the freedom we have to purchase and read the Scriptures. Those who work with Gideons International who place Bibles in hotels, schools and prisons fulfil a wonderful ministry and are certainly worthy of our support. We would be wrong however to therefore assume that the Church is good at making the gospel accessible simply because it is good at making it available. There is a world of difference.

Only a small minority of people in the UK attend a place of worship. A survey taken in 2007 showed that three million people in Britain, who do not currently attend church, would be willing to do so if invited with courtesy. It did not say that they would commit to become a Christian or promise to go regularly: simply that they would attend if asked.

Let us suppose that in the space of one year the three million people found themselves for the first time in church. We have to ask ourselves to what degree would they be exposed to a message that would offer the transformation that would lead them to eternal life and to a deep and lasting encounter with God?

Even were such a seismic change to take place in church attendance patterns, this would still leave millions outside the church's orbit.

Jonah had been reluctant to travel to Nineveh to call the population to repent. He had to be thrown overboard then swallowed by a great fish before he offered up a prayer of penitence and was back on course again.

We all know, however, that having a message to take, and even a willingness to transmit it, does not mean that the truth will therefore be communicated.

Jonah eventually became the catalyst in a revival that touched every individual and penetrated every section of society. This was not accomplished, however, by hiring a hall and sending out leaflets to say that he would be speaking at 11 a.m. and 7 p.m. every Sunday on Nineveh's sins.

This is not at all to say that Christian meetings serve no future purpose – of course they do. The problem is that they are Christian meetings – held by Christians and, most often, for the benefit of Christians.

We have seen in previous chapters the importance of community involvement in communicating the heart of God to those in our locality. For those of us who believe that the spiritual gifts of 1 Corinthians 12 – 14 are relevant for today – these should be used exponentially more in the public square than the church if the New Testament is our model.

As we read the book of Acts we discover more people ministered to in the equivalent of the shopping mall than we do in the precincts of the temple.

Earlier in this book I drew attention to a secular agenda to marginalise the Church. However, it has to be said that the biggest danger that the Church faces is its own marginalisation of itself. Our failure to be salt and light, combined with a propensity to retreat behind the self-imposed barricades of personal blessing, put the onus more at our door than that of the devil.

On one occasion my wife and I were enjoying an excellent Indian meal at a restaurant in downtown Glasgow. Our minds were not at all on 'ministry' but on relaxing with our friends. Out of the corner of my eye I noticed a tall man of African descent leave the table where he had been sitting with his girlfriend and walk to the buffet to serve himself. As he did so I felt God clearly speak to me about his life.

Excusing myself from the table I crossed over to where he was and approached him. I asked if his name was Michael and he said that it was. I inquired if he was from Nigeria and he said that was correct. I asked if he was raised in the town of Ibadan and he told me that that was where he was born and raised. It was clear that I now had his attention! I then went on to relate to him the word that I felt God had for his life.

If the preacher is the postman then the person using spiritual gifts brings the message by special delivery.

To have invited Michael to attend the next meeting at a local church in a few days' time would have been inappropriate to say the least.

To confine the bringing of a word from God, or the demonstration of the power of God, to a geographical location where the non-Christian must assemble before it can be applied is almost too ridiculous to contemplate. Yet the Church puts those limiting parameters on the exercise of spiritual gifts all the time and considers it the norm.

When Philip was called by God from a revival into the desert in order to find the Ethiopian equivalent of the Chancellor of the Exchequer, we read that the man's chariot was travelling away from Jerusalem.[8] Many people's 'chariots' are moving away from 'where the church is'. They have not rejected God, or the person of Jesus, but the church is increasingly an irrelevance to them. To argue that they are wrong in their view is to entirely miss the point. They are travelling in a different direction. Philip met him where he was and by the time the man had reached his home he had already been baptised into the faith.

Richard and Rajindark Buxton lead Ealing Christian Centre, an Elim church with a Sunday attendance of well over a thousand people. Their services are powerful and many hundreds of people are personally impacted by the ministry of this dynamic local church every week.

Some leaders would be satisfied to lead such a vibrant congregation but the Buxtons felt that, even with a thriving church, their spiritual impact on their community near the heart of London was minimal.

Bigger People are not satisfied with shallow horizons.

The church decided to ask permission from the local council to place tables and chairs outside a busy thoroughfare with a view to offering prayer and counsel to any who passed by. Permission was subsequently granted. As a result, shoppers who asked for personal prayer, and who may never have considered darkening the door of a church, were ministered to on their own territory. Several testified to having been healed as a result of prayer as church members (not just church leaders) sensitively served them by praying with them and for them.

It should be added that all those who were involved had been well prepared by personal prayer and were people of credibility and personal integrity working under the auspices of the local church. None were novices. All, however, were open to be used by God and all were surprised by the willingness of people to engage with them. Some of those on the streets said that this was the first time in their entire lives that anyone had offered to pray with them.

None of us would surely argue that those, who have no Christians within their friends or family circle, must wait until they are invited to attend a meeting of Christians on a certain day, in an appropriate place and at a specified time before they can receive anything from God.

That we have operated like this for so long is frightening. The argument is not that every church service should be conducted in the open. It is just that they should simply be recognised for what they are – services for the church. Our testimony is tested in the context of the office and the factory – so why not allow the miraculous to accompany us as well?

Credibility

Even the most unfair criticism can carry within it a grain of truth. The assertion 'the Church is full of hypocrites' is palpably not true but the fact that the watching world expects authenticity from Christians is incontrovertible.

When the local butcher runs off with another man's wife it does not make the papers. When the local vicar does the same thing it hits the headlines. The Lord Jesus does not have to earn the right to speak – he has already done so. His Church, however, has to.

Sincerity cannot be measured in decibels. To say a Christian 'sounds so sincere' is insufficient evidence – something far more tangible is required.

The word sincere (*sine cere*) literally means 'without wax'. The word was forged in an era when the primary status symbol in affluent homes was a stone bust made in honour of the head of the household.

Unscrupulous stonemasons, rather than owning up to substandard work and thereby getting a fraction of the price, would endeavour to cover up their mistakes by sealing broken areas with wax. They knew it was almost impossible to see the join with the naked eye.

Even the most discerning customers could be easily deceived and so, before parting with payment, they would take the bust out into the sunlight and subject it to the heat of the sun. If glue had been applied it would very quickly be apparent as a nose or ear fell away under the rising temperature. If it stood the test it was declared to be without wax – totally sincere.

One of the most difficult truths for many of us to accept is why 'bad things happen to good people'. This is especially true when those who are suffering are our family or friends. It is a recurring theme throughout Scripture.

Credibility and integrity are most often displayed in the crucible of suffering or the wind tunnel of inordinate seasons of stress.

Emerging intact from the far side of the furnace is a witness more articulate than any sermon. Signs and wonders are not just instantaneous miracles that fall from heaven. I can name many of them: they are people I know. When I think of them I marvel and truly believe that I could not have endured as they have done. They talk of sufficient grace. It is something available to us all – the divine asbestos for every fiery trial.

And of course there is the place where credibility come under fire via temptation. It wasn't a walkover for Jesus so it is not going to be a walkover for the rest of us. The writer of the book of Hebrews tells that he suffered being tempted.[9]

It is easy to limit the overcoming of temptation to a 'St George and the Dragon' encounter. We all know that the theatre of battle is very much wider than that. It is not all about set-piece struggles. The Lord Jesus encourages us to pray that we are not led into temptation and that we be delivered from evil. This reveals to us that there is preventative grace and restraining grace as well as the grace that accompanies forgiveness.

Relevance

Few things excite me more than seeing the Christian message presented coherently, intelligently and relevantly.

When I was a pastor I was asked by a member of my congregation to visit a lady who lived in a home for the elderly. When I arrived and gave the name of the person I wanted to see the receptionist greeted me with a look of mild bemusement. As we walked together to the day room she said that this must obviously have been my first visit and suggested to me that she did not think it would be likely that I would be there very long.

I took from this that the lady I was to see was probably profoundly deaf and that it was this that was likely to cut my visit short if not make it totally fruitless.

The person I was visiting turned out to be in her sixties, well dressed, with a beautiful smile and not at all deaf. As I introduced myself I immediately discovered what the problem was. Due to a brain disorder she only had one word in her vocabulary to which she answered every question.

I was later to be told that she understood perfectly what I was saying and she had no problem framing the reply in her mind. The problem was that as she mentally constructed her response, she thought that the one word she repeated was a cogent reply and expected me to understand it. While sympathizing greatly with her, my anxiety was tempered by the fact that she remained unaware, and therefore unperturbed by her condition. In the case of this lovely lady this eventuality was a blessing. In the case of the Church it is not.

When I am abroad I try to use as much of the local language as I am able. My attempts are usually pitiful in most places but at least I am aware that I am not communicating well and embarrassed that I am not more fluent.

My new friend, through no fault of her own, was blissfully unaware of her failure to communicate. And that so often is a problem with the Church.

Where do we suppose the idea ever came from that, depending upon ecclesiastical background, in order to find their way to the most important truth in the world, people are required to first hack their way through a glossary of evangelical jargon, Elizabethan English and, in some cases Latin. I can't believe that was ever God's idea.

This is not about 'dumbing down' or being cool. It is about waking up and getting real.

Just because the Church is able to speak does not mean that its voice remains intact and its message is coherent.

Getting heard in heaven

If the Church fails to be heard on Earth – that's bad. If we fail to be heard in heaven – that's fatal.

There are those who believe that God listens to every prayer. Not only is that not the case but he has gone to great lengths in the Scriptures to tell us five reasons why.

(i) Iniquity issues
'If I had cherished sin in my heart, the Lord would not have listened'.[10] One paraphrase adds, 'If I am cosy with evil.'

We need to note that the Bible does not say that God goes deaf – for that would be a weakness to which deity cannot be prone. It is simply that God makes a conscious choice not to listen to us in those circumstances – a frightening thought.

Nor does this mean that God only listens to those who live totally pristine and inerrant existences. Were that to be the case no one would ever be heard.

The picture is of sin that we hold onto and refuse to renounce. It refers to that which we clutch to ourselves erecting a barricade around it, and creating a no-go area for God. When that situation obtains the dreadful words in Romans 1 begin to apply. The conscience is seared with an iron and not only does God not hear us; we cease to hear him.

If I go to my doctor and complain of pains in my chest and he recommends a change in exercise and diet, he expects me to hear him. If I return in a month's time complaining of the same symptoms he is likely to ask me if I have changed to the regime that he had suggested. If I were to respond to the effect that I would like fresh instructions that are more palatable, he is likely to suggest that he will not speak again on the matter until I have implemented what he has already said. Any further entreaties from me are likely to fall on 'deaf ears'. The assumption is not that he has deficient hearing: the issue of deficiency in that case would entirely lie with me.

The Message says 'God has no use for the prayers of the people who won't listen to him.'[11]

(ii) Integrity issues

'When you ask, you do not receive, because you ask with wrong motives'.[12]

Why we want what we want is far more important than *what* we want. When the Scriptures say that all our work will be tested by fire[13] it is motivation more than activity that will come under scrutiny.

The difference between motivation and manipulation is that, in the first instance, we are seeking to inspire someone to move towards God's best plan for their lives. Manipulation has to do with using other people to fulfil our dreams and aspirations.

Motive in the case of petitioning in prayer is tested against a similar benchmark.

(iii) Equity issues

'If a man shuts his ears to the cry of the poor, he too will cry out and not be answered.'[14]

I believe that how we handle our money is one of the most difficult areas that the Christian has to address and it is something that can only be settled between an individual and God.

It has been said that 25 per cent of the teaching of Jesus has to do with our possessions and we live in a world in which 25 per cent of the population has to survive on less than £2 per week.

Big People need to have the largeness of spirit to come to their own conclusions without making negative appraisals on lifestyles of the others. The criteria on which we come to such personal decisions have to do with both proportion and perspective.

On my first ministry visit to the United States in the early eighties I was hosted by the one of the leaders of a well-known group of churches. I had hardly been in his magnificent home for more than a few minutes when he enquired as to how much I earned. I was surprised by the question but, as my salary was a matter of record, I saw no reason not to tell him. He appeared aghast and responded to the effect that ministers in his denomination received more in utility expenses than I received in my total income.

Within a few days of my return home we had a Christian leader from India staying with us. It was his first visit to the west and the culture shock was hitting him hard. He asked me how much a colour TV licence was, and when I told him, he said it was the same amount as a village worker's annual salary. On seeing a commercial for pet food he was astounded not only by the cost but by that fact that animals should be given anything but scraps. He was later to refuse cream at lunch on the basis of 'But think how many gospel tracts the cream could buy!'

Days earlier I was told I was living as a pauper and now I was now considered to be living like a prince. The fact is, depending on where we live in the world, both assertions could be considered to be true.

I have friends who live sacrificial lifestyles that release significant proportions of their income to missions. I have friends in the developing world who do not have the luxury of choice in their standard of living and who live on the edge of poverty.

I also number among my friends those who are extremely wealthy, who live in luxurious homes and drive the most expensive cars. I am also aware that were anyone to add up the money they have given to ministry, in some cases, it would be measured in millions of pounds.

The oft-neglected Romans 14 is the correct lens through which this issue should be viewed.

Paul speaks of those who eat certain foods and others who refrain from a similar diet. He talks of those who hold certain days special and those that do not. He rightly recoils from the temptation to make choices for others and argues that each of us is answerable only to God. Unfortunately, Christians are all too adept at legislating for the consciences of fellow Christians based on decisions that they have made for themselves.

I hear one section of the Church argue that rich nations should write off the debt of poorer countries and another say that, until endemic corruption is addressed, such stances are naïve given that those who are the poorest would not be helped.

I have heard Christian leaders criticised for staying in comfortable hotels in the developing world which are out of reach of those to whom they are ministering. I have listened to the response that asks if it is sensible to travel halfway around the world only to be incapacitated by infected water and unsanitary conditions.

Smith Wigglesworth, renowned as the apostle of faith, came from a northern, blue collar background. Throughout his ministry he received criticism for wearing good clothes and travelling in comfort. One detractor had at least the courage to challenge him to his face when he discovered that he had travelled by train to a meeting in a first-class carriage. To the accusation, 'Do you not think that such profligacy is a waste of the Lord's money?' he replied, 'What do you think the Lord would prefer to waste – his money or his servants?'

The media usually takes a perverse stance on this matter. A TV interviewer asked Billy Graham why he had sailed to Britain on the Queen Mary when Jesus went into Jerusalem on a donkey. Graham responded 'If you can find a donkey that can swim the Atlantic, we will buy it.'

Over his long and rich ministry the media have scrutinised Dr Graham's lifestyle in an effort to bring him into disrepute. Despite their every effort, the integrity of this spiritual statesman remains intact.

The 'God wants you rich' message of the prosperity teachers might resonate with those who argue that unless we have wealth we are unable to provide for the needs of others.

The Christian living in slavery in the Sudan, or one of the tens of thousands undergoing unspeakable cruelty in North Korea, has a different prosperity message that witnesses, 'Because I refused to renounce my faith in Christ, I lost my job, my wealth, my health, my family and my freedom.'

The biblical perspective is that those who are financially blessed should not covet more for its own sake while, at the same time, acting responsibly with what they have. Nor should they live with guilt because of the blessing that God has granted them.

The Apostle Paul knew what it was to abound and also to suffer want[15] but was willing to be content in whatever state he found himself. This did not mean that, when in need, he was not expectant of increased provision nor grateful for it when it came. It meant that he refused to waste his energies in avarice or jealousy and focussed on fulfilling the purposes of God within his current means.

(iv) Ego issues
'clothe yourselves with humility towards one another, because, "God opposes the proud but gives grace to the humble."'[16]

The Amplified Bible puts it this way, 'For God sets Himself against the proud (the insolent, the overbearing, the disdainful, the presumptuous, the boastful) – [and He opposes, frustrates, and defeats them], but gives grace (favor, blessing) to the humble.'

There are those that take the view that true humility is a form of verbal self-degradation in the presence of others. The Chinese leader Watchman Nee, who lived nearly a century ago, wrote in his book *Spiritual Man* that humility is not a looking down on oneself: rather it is not looking at oneself at all. He wrote that we must have a spirit of power towards the enemy, a spirit of love towards men, and a spirit of self-control towards ourselves.[17]

The words humour and humility derive from the same root. Humility is not denying our strengths but about being honest about our weaknesses. It is certainly to do with not taking ourselves too seriously.

John Maxwell mirrors this perspective when he said that at his funeral his friends would tell heart-warming stories and give generous eulogies but, twenty minutes later at the meal, the most important thing on their minds will be to find out who had got the potato salad.[18]

As infants we are not blessed with a wide vocabulary and so, believing ourselves to be the centre of the universe, we scream and shout until we attract sufficient attention to get our way. Some people carry on a similar game well into adulthood.

John Ortberg observes that there was no grandiosity in Jesus and that was why people had such a hard time recognizing him for who he was. He goes on to say that every human who has ever lived has suffered from the Messiah complex except one – and he was called the Messiah.

It has been said that EGO simply means, 'edging God out'.

In a remarkable demonstration of humility, the Israelite women gave their brass looking-glasses to be melted down to fashion the laver for the Temple.[19] Their action demonstrated the fact that what had been a means of reflecting their own beauty prior to meeting others was transformed into a place for spiritual preparation prior to coming before God.

(v) Family issues

> Husbands, in the same way be considerate as you live with your wives, and treat them with respect as the weaker partner and as heirs with you of the gracious gift of life, so that nothing will hinder your prayers.[20] (*The Message* paraphrases 'hinder' as 'running aground')

The issue is bigger than the responsibilities of the husband and wife or even of marriage itself. One of the core messages of this verse is the parallel between marriage and our relationship with God – if we are not willing to listen to one another why should we imagine that God will listen to us?

The response to the disciples' inquiry about how they should pray (that resulted in what we have come to know as the Lord's Prayer) came with a statement that appeared to go beyond the bounds of instruction about intercession. 'If you forgive your brother, I will forgive you. If you will not forgive your brother I will not forgive you'.[21]

It is said that Leonardo Da Vinci was in the middle of painting a very important picture which centred around the face of Jesus, when a group of boys came to visit him. While they were there, one inadvertently knocked over a stack of canvasses. In an angry response to the perceived clumsiness, Leonardo became angry and threw his brush and a few harsh words at the lad who subsequently ran crying from the studio. When all the children had left and calm had been restored he went back to work but, try as he might, he could not continue the picture. Eventually, putting down his brush he went outside into the streets until he found the boy and apologised for his anger. Returning to the studio he was able to finish the masterpiece that later was to became an inspiration to millions.

C.S. Lewis wrote, 'To be a Christian means to forgive the inexcusable, because God has forgiven the inexcusable in you.'[22]

There is an amazing passage in 1 Samuel that encapsulates all that is meant by having a voice that is heard on earth and in heaven.

> The LORD was with Samuel as he grew up, and he let none of his words fall to the ground. And all Israel . . . recognised that Samuel was attested as a prophet of the LORD [*The Message* paraphrases this phrase as 'recognised that he was the real thing']. The LORD continued to

appear at Shiloh, and there he revealed himself to Samuel through his word.[23]

Whenever I read this I imagine an arrow flying from heaven, penetrating Samuel and then travelling on to impact those to whom he was called to minister.

A Church that hears clearly what God is saying – and has the ability to transmit the message unfiltered, unpolluted and unsullied with personal agenda – is a Church that will be heard both on earth and in heaven.

4

Generational Blessing

Bigger People possess the capacity to see beyond the horizons that mark the limiting parameters of the average Christian.

The biblical teaching of generational blessing amplifies the importance of making decisions in the here and now that will continue to have an effect in the medium to long-term. It stretches far beyond what can be seen today, into the heart of what God has for tomorrow.

We currently live in a small hamlet in the Cotswolds. There are no street lights. As I switch on my car ignition in the early morning before daylight has broken my headlights will penetrate only a few metres into the darkness ahead of me. It would be unthinkable not to engage either gear or accelerator until my destination was fully in sight.

Three things are immediately assumed. The first is that I know where I am going and my destination is clear to me. The second is that, although I am currently in the dark, there are likely to be landmarks on the way that I am anticipating and will be reference points as I travel. Thirdly, I am confident that as I begin to move the vision provided by my headlights will move proportionately with me.

Assuming that the entire journey will be in the dark, my headlights will not rest on my destination until a few moments before I finally arrive.

When the psalmist said, 'Your word is a lamp to my feet and a light for my path'[1] two things would be known by him.

The first was that, unlike the car headlights, the burning torch shone as much, if not more, on the person carrying it as it did on the path. The second is that revelation increases in direct proportion to the willingness of the torch-bearer to advance into the light they have already received.

The first prophecy ever uttered was spoken by God, not to man, but to the serpent.[2] God said, 'I will put enmity between you and the woman, and between your offspring and hers; he will crush your head, and you will strike his heel.' The light of revelation shone into a present fulfilment but, in the mind of God, also stretched through the darkness of thousands of years to the eventual fulfilment in the victory of the cross.

God always sees beyond. We think with a family perspective and live from day to day. God thinks generationally. Over 160 times this term is used in Scripture. It is abundantly clear that the God who will 'make all things new'[3] is also the 'Ancient of Days'.[4]

In Exodus it says that 'the LORD has commanded: "Take an omer of manna and keep it for the generations to come, so they can see the bread I gave you to eat in the desert when I brought you out of Egypt."'[5]

Though to most people at the time the account of the miraculous provision of manna, this was nothing more than, 'getting my needs met in the here and now' God was looking much further.

Bigger People see beyond. When Esau in Genesis 25 sold his birthright for a bowl of stew his twin's vision was not limited in this way. Though his methods left something to be desired his mother, who instigated the ruse, had the future in view and did not suffer from the malaise of myopia that confines such a large section of the Church in its quest for short-term blessing.

Generational Blessing is about going deep

On one occasion when preaching at a conference in Phoenix, Arizona the outside temperature regularly reached over a hundred degrees in the desert. I did not see rain for the entire time I was there but was told that there were regular times when the 'heavens opened' with torrents of refreshing water hurtling towards the arid ground. The problem was that the water only engaged the environment superficially.

It was at that point that I was first introduced to the term gully-washer which described the hard-baked ditches that carried the needed water away. There was no question of a refreshing river running; the problem was that the water never got deep enough to produce the saturation needed for growth. As soon as the downpour ended, any remnants of refreshment that were left evaporated rapidly under the desert sun.

I have been in meetings like that. Perhaps you have too. The blessing is real and there is a palpable sense of the presence of God. The problem was that I never opened up wide enough. I failed to let it soak through. I was the recipient of blessing that touched me but failed to change me. What then transpired was that, when the atmosphere changed, all that had touched me dissolved and was wasted.

Showers of blessing are only half the answer. What matters most is that the soil on which they fall has furrows deep enough to retain something beyond today –

something that will be the precursor of tomorrow's harvest.

When the Pilgrim Fathers landed in America it is said that in the first year they established a town. During the second year they established a town council. The following year the population impeached the town council as the council had had the temerity to want to spend money constructing a road into the wilderness. How quickly intrepid adventurers became settlers, and pioneers whose vision had been focussed on a tomorrow, become consumed by the shallow fulfilment supplied by today.

In a previous book I highlighted the fact that in Genesis we read of Terah, Abraham's father, setting out from Ur of the Chaldeans to go to Canaan but then deciding to settle in Haran.[6] It appears that Terah lived until he was 205. Later Abraham set out again and arrived – but what about the time that had been wasted? It is like setting out on a motorway journey but spending 150 years at a service station.

Generational Blessing is about being a father (or mother)

Bigger People are committed to build largeness in the lives of others and thinking beyond their own personal dreams and desire for blessing.

Paul refers to himself as a mentor, a mother and a father.[7]

The most powerful passage in this regard is:

> For though you might have ten thousand instructors in Christ, yet you do not have many fathers; for in Christ Jesus I have begotten you through the gospel. Therefore I urge you, imitate me. For this reason I have sent

Timothy to you, who is my beloved and faithful son in the Lord, who will remind you of my ways in Christ, as I teach everywhere in every church.[8]

The genes from our biological parents dictate that we resemble them physically. The genetics of influence that we exercise as spiritual mothers and fathers can have a major influence on the lives of others and determine the kind of people they eventually become. Note that I said 'can' and not 'should'. The problem is that this influence can have both positive and negative effects.

Cult leaders have taken disciples under their wing and created dangerous clones of themselves to the degree that their influence takes on a sinister form of spiritual abuse.

There are even biblical accounts of natural fathers whose negative traits become replicated in their offspring.

Abraham was aware that his wife was so beautiful that others might also be attracted to her and that this would perhaps create a threat to him – especially if they were powerful people. In Genesis we read how he made a decision to pass her off as his sister and, in consequence, Abimelech, king of Gerah, would have taken her for himself had not God intervened on Sarah's behalf.[9]

That this was a huge lapse in integrity for Abraham was not the primary issue. The problem was that this was not an isolated incident. The very same thing had happened before:

As he was about to enter Egypt, he said to his wife Sarai, "I know what a beautiful woman you are. When the Egyptians see you, they will say, 'This is his wife.' Then

they will kill me but will let you live. Say you are my sister, so that I will be treated well for your sake and my life
will be spared because of you."[10]

Sadly, when Abraham's son Isaac finds himself in a similar situation he resorts to exactly the same deceit. 'So
Abimelech summoned Isaac and said, "She is really
your wife! Why did you say, 'She is my sister'?" Isaac
answered him, "Because I thought I might lose my life
on account of her."'[11]

Nowhere else in Scripture is such a ploy recorded and
most of us would not have heard of such a tactic used in
any other context. It is more than a coincidence that it is
found three times within the same family.

This is the shadow-side of the subject and serves as a
warning. The positive aspect is found in Paul's relationship with Timothy. We notice that, though he acknowledges him as a 'son in the faith' he also respects the spiritual DNA that has flowed through his biological family
– the influence of mother and grandmother. Nor does he
suggest that this positive pervasive influence in any way
absolves Timothy from a commitment to his own personal development:

> I have been reminded of your sincere faith, which first
> lived in your grandmother Lois and in your mother
> Eunice and, I am persuaded, now lives in you also. For
> this reason I remind you to fan into flame the gift of
> God, which is in you through the laying on of my
> hands.[12]

Bigger People, in looking beyond their own blessings,
gifts and aspiration, look to be parents to spiritual sons
and daughters who will replicate and reproduce a
spiritual inheritance.

There are three primary strands to this genetic code:

1. Modelling a good example;
2. Speaking positive words of affirmation;
3. Telling the truth in love where correction is needed.

A recent survey revealed that 50 per cent of fathers in the United Kingdom spend less than five minutes per day in one-to-one quality time with their children. Little wonder therefore that we have such a high proportion of dysfunctional families and damaged children.

The Church, with its eye to passing on its influence generationally, must at all cost create a fabric of relationship so that the local congregation is not just a fellowship in name only.

A church that fails to grasp this does so at its peril. Church leaders are not primarily called to be CEOs of organisations, land-locked behind desks and umbiblically connected to computers. They are heads of spiritual families. Clearly senior ministers pastoring large congregations cannot hope to personally connect with every single member of the church. However, they must at all cost ensure there is a network of connectivity which people can join.

People come to church more for warmth than light. If good teaching is all that is needed, they can get that through Christian TV and websites. I occasionally meet people who have said that there is so little sense of connection in the local church, with its cliques and insular self-interest, that making the journey to it (with the hassle it entails) is simply not worth it.

Kensington Temple in London is several thousand in number yet retains a sense of care and fellowship through its network of cells. Senior Pastor, Colin Dye, has ensured that smallness at the heart of largeness is part of its core vision and values. Though its worship and music teams are of the utmost quality and the teaching is of the highest standard, those who attend are neither audience nor even congregation but the body of the church. Fitting into a framework designed for growth that lasts, new converts quickly move into a discipleship environment that guides them towards long-term spiritual maturity.

Generational blessing, through whatever means it is cultivated, is God's heart for his Church and where it is evident the following truth becomes a reality:

> Your sons will take the place of your fathers; you will make them princes throughout the land. I will perpetuate your memory through all generations; therefore the nations will praise you for ever and ever.[13]

5

The Home of the Heart

There are several analogies of Church in the Scriptures. body, building and bride are the most quoted yet there are many others ranging from the fellowship of family to the fertility of a field.

Jesus used parables in order to make spiritual ideas more tangible but also so that we could make sense of infinite ideas by concentrating our focus on finite stories.

In the first psalm the individual believer, rather than the corporate Church, is encouraged to momentarily step outside of a reality in which they see themselves as flesh and blood and mentally transform themselves into an inanimate object. The Holy Spirit inspires him to say that the righteous man was 'like a tree'. Seven hundred years later Jesus will use a similar analogy as he makes a correlation between vine and branches. The principle remains the same and it is remarkable what happens when we try and conceptualise our spiritual state in something other than the standard jargon normally employed.

In my early years in ministry I attended a course on clinical psychology. These were small group seminars that usually took the form of teaching followed by discussion and interaction. One week, however, was different – on that occasion the leader of the group disconcertingly asked us to close our eyes and imagine that we were rose bushes.

As a young man brought up in a working-class area in northern England this mental metamorphis did not come easily. I was well aware what rose bushes were but the thought that I should entertain the idea of being one was something of a challenge. However, for the sake of the moment, I fought back my initial cynicism and went along with it as best I could.

When at the end we were invited to share with the group what we had seen my initial inclination was to assume that this would be a repetitive exercise in which, though there might be slight variations in size and colour, there would be little variation in the descriptions – well, how different can a rose bush be?

I was to be proved wrong.

The descriptions were widely different and when people later recounted their personal stories it was clear that normal mental defence mechanisms (that allow us to adjust our self-image according to the views of others and even ourselves) had been bypassed or at least temporarily suspended.

My 'rose bush' had reflected one that I remembered in the garden of my childhood home. Another in the group appeared amazed that the rest of us had considered a rose bush in a planted context at all. His first thought, it transpired, had been a rose bush potted in a garden centre, covered in a plastic bag and offered for sale. We later learned his story – he had been abandoned as a child, grew up in an orphanage and had eventually married but had yet to really put down lasting roots, either geographically or emotionally.

Fifteen years later I was conducting a residential retreat for a group of pastors in Scotland. We had finished the sessions for the day and were relaxing in the lounge. As my friends and colleagues chatted the subject touched on the inner life of the leader. A few hours previously, when preparing for the final session, I had thought of the rose bush incident and consequently felt prompted to suggest that we do something entirely different to what we had planned for the evening.

I had wondered what the reaction would be but it soon became clear that my friends were wired-up far less cynically than me and were happy to engage with whatever God might want to say to them.

We turned to Psalm 1 and I first asked everyone to meditate for a few minutes with an open Bible. We then shared what we felt the Lord was saying, in a general sense, through the verses. It is sometimes far easier to generalise Scripture than allow it to relate specifically to the way we live. Human nature being what it is, there is always a danger of intellectualising revelation and thus keeping it at arm's length.

What was to happen next was far more revelatory but, first of all it might be helpful to address the idea of meditation.

There are people in the Christian Church with whom I would also include myself, that have never taken the idea of meditation seriously. The fact is, however, that we are encouraged far more in Scripture to meditate on the word of God than simply to 'read our Bibles'. Meditation is even looked upon with suspicion by some in the belief that it really only belongs to religions whose practices are based in eastern mysticism. It surely isn't for Christians – especially evangelical ones – and particularly those of a Pentecostal or charismatic disposition.

As far as our approach to the Bible is concerned, we are sometimes more concerned with reading a prescribed number of chapters per day. It is almost as if we have set ourselves a challenge that must be endured. At the end of the daily exercise we may feel good that we have kept to the discipline but if we were asked what God had said to us, we might sometimes be at a loss to offer a cogent reply.

It is a little like visiting an art gallery. Had we thirty minutes to spare we could use them running into the entrance, power-walking past the paintings, sprinting from floor to floor and emerging out of the exit with a satisfied smile that says we've 'done the whole place'. On the other hand, we could spend the entire half hour standing in front of one masterpiece, looking for things we have never seen before, admiring light on landscape and the intricate effects of delicate brush stokes.

The former depicts Bible reading at its worst and the latter is an account of meditation at its best.

Meditation takes time. When I think of it I am drawn to the story of a Victorian manager of a colliery who attended the same chapel as the miners who worked deep underground. They were different in every way imaginable and the social class conventions of the day meant that manager and miners rarely met. A particular bond between the manager and one of his workers was created by their common Christian faith. The manager would sometimes visit this man's cottage when taking a stroll through his village.

On one occasion the miner was found sitting in his chair reading his Bible and when the manager asked which chapter he was reading he was told, Romans 8. On the next visit the same thing happened and the question elicited the same response.

'But you were in Romans 8 the last time I called.'

'I know,' said the miner, 'It's just that I decided to sink a shaft there.'

That is meditation. Jesus spoke of the wise man who brought out of his treasures things both old and new. In this context we might say that previously learned truths are the 'things old' whereas revelations gleaned through meditation are 'things new'.

Bigger People allocate time to hear God at a deeper level. They will not be satisfied with superficial engagement with Scripture any more than they will allow prayer to denigrate into the presentation of personal shopping lists before a deity whose sole role in the universe is to sort out their life for them – a kind of cosmic butler.

But now let's return to the account of the pastors' retreat and the time that was spent around the first psalm.

Once everyone had shared their thoughts on the passage relating to the believer as a tree I suggested that everyone close their eyes and imagine that the tree that they were now contemplating was their own spiritual condition. As they did so I asked them to describe to themselves what they were seeing and I offered some pointers that included:

- What condition is the tree in?
- What are the bark and the branches like?
- Are there leaves on the tree?
- Is the tree bearing fruit?
- What season is the tree in: autumn, winter, spring or summer?
- Where is the tree in relation to other trees?
- What of the roots – are they near the stream/s or far away?
- What of the stream – was it deep or shallow, clear or murky, running or stagnant?

These are only some of the questions that were posed but there are far more than most would have imagined necessary from a cursory consideration of the text.

When the exercise was over and people were chatting about their individual trees I noticed that one of our group was missing. I was not overly concerned as it was getting late and I assumed that the pastor in question had retired to his room for the night.

It was only after I was heading off to my own room that I found him sitting on his own in the corner of a lounge. My colleague was someone always known for his positive disposition. His church was always 'going well' whenever anyone asked about it, and any inquiry was couched with superlatives whenever his ministry was mentioned.

Tonight had been different. His filters had been temporarily bypassed and the reflex reaction of a positive response was absent. He had encountered reality and described to me a tree in winter, stripped bare of bark and vulnerable, without a stream in sight. This was reality and God had reached him by side-stepping the semantics associated with flimsy faith statements.

In the forty years I have been a pastor I have discovered that disillusionment in ministry usually commences with a false illusion in the first instance. In this case it was someone who felt that he had to appear as successful even when he was feeling depressed. By masking his ministry with a smile he had come to the remarkable conclusion that this plastic posture was somehow glorifying to God.

At last he was in a place where God could come close enough to heal. He had entered a place we should all be in yet too often withdraw from.

Meditation involves looking, listening, analysis and application. In the section that follows we are going to ask the question, 'If our heart was a house: what condition would it be in?'

The Lounge

In the home that I grew up in this area was off-limits to the children and usually used only when guests arrived. Some of my friends called it the sitting room or the drawing room but, however it was named, it was always empty of toys and always kept immaculate, with not a cushion out of place.

Visitors were 'received' in the room and rarely ventured elsewhere unless they were staying for supper. In those days, only close family friends would have felt at ease following my parents into other areas of the house. It was almost as if people had security passes that were valid only in designated areas. Nothing of course was said. It was just intuitively known.

The TV programme *Through the Keyhole*, chaired by Sir David Frost, was compelling viewing for some. Lloyd Grossman would wander around celebrity homes dropping the occasional clue as to its inhabitant. It was up to a panel to decide who the occupant might be, based on the various social signals that had been sent out. On those occasions the whole house became a lounge – just as one might expect when millions of viewers became virtual voyeurs for the duration of the program. No one ever witnessed a potato peeling or unwashed cutlery in the kitchen. Beds were always made and the garden, if ever it was shown, was perpetually free of weeds.

All of us have lounge areas in our lives. We 'share our heart' at various levels and instinctively know who we can allow to come close and who should be held at a distance. A certain conversation with one person is considered intimate but with another intrusive. With a close friend we can go almost anywhere their thoughts take them while an acquaintance can easily cross a line reserved only for those whose security passes grant them admission – gained by trust or the relationship's longevity.

Of course, the lounge area is never who we really are. It solely about how we wish to be perceived. This presentation of the persona is rarely a deceit that offers others a false image. It is more often concerned with a reserve that is reticent to be totally transparent. In fairness, its in-built control orders are more often rooted in wisdom than guile.

The Kitchen

Were you to scrutinise our kitchen and examine the contents of our cupboards, it would not take you long to come to a conclusion about our diet. You would soon be aware of how wholesome you believed it was – or wasn't. You may not gain a prefect picture but you would come away with a pretty good idea.

Bigger People are careful about what they consume – they are concerned about nutritional content and the presence of additives.

Fast food

We have already looked at the two most obvious areas of input – meditation and prayer – and have noted the need to guard against superficial spirituality if we are to experience success as well as survival. There appears to be reluctance in our current culture to refer to such things as 'disciplines'. This is especially true in some Christian circles which view any attempt to order one's life as teetering on the edge of legalism and in opposition to grace. Discipline, however, is considered cool if you are an athlete or in training for a marathon. Most things of value come with a degree of cost and climbing high rarely comes without a degree of effort.

Toxicity

The most important spiritual discipline I ever engaged in was to go on a media fast. I conducted it for three months during which time I did not watch anything, including the TV news. I was a pastor at the time and, unbeknown to me, my worship leader did the same thing (though for a shorter period). During that time, our whole church entered an entirely different spiritual plane.

I became aware that I had been drinking from a polluted stream. Not because I had been watching R-rated movies but just because I was being constantly 'fed' a steady stream of data from a world-view that was, for the most part, ungodly in source and content.

It was as if previously I had been a long-distance rambler who had been hiking through the wilderness and, when looking for refreshment, taking water from a river in which all manner of toxic pollutants had been dumped upstream.

A fast like this does not have to last for three months – just long enough to get the toxicity out of the system.

Sugar-buzz spirituality

When I am travelling it is far easier to grab a coffee and doughnut than sit down to a healthy meal. Not a good idea I know, but it provides the short-term satisfaction that springs from the sugar-buzz or the caffeine rush. The sensation of course is deceptive and does not sustain us in the long term. Before long we need another shot and end up far fatter than fitter.

When Esau exchanged his destiny for fast food he became an icon for myopia – short-sightedness. Instant gratification, in whatever form it takes, means we end up losing a lot more than we ever gain.

I once had a framed picture in my office of a conductor leading an orchestra. It showed the musicians and the conductor's back. The caption beneath it read, 'To produce great music, you sometimes have to turn your back on the crowd.'

Leaders who are pastoral, or people-orientated, sometimes find it hard to make decisions that, while right, may not necessarily be popular. The fear of what people think has led to many ineffectual decisions that have stunted both growth and blessing. Good leaders do not dominate and, whenever possible, want to carry the willing support of those they are seeking to serve. On some occasions those same leaders may be required to grasp the nettle and make choices that are based on principle rather than consensus.

Humanity, and that includes all of us, have a potential to be fickle. When the Apostle Paul was shipwrecked on the island of Malta and a serpent rose from the fire to attack him, the onlookers assumed that he must be a notorious criminal. Their logic was that, having escaped drowning, tenacious fate had conspired to exact judgement on him. Minutes later when it was clear that he had not succumbed to the anticipated catastrophe, he was then deemed to be divine.

The applause of the crowd, while welcome, should not become an objective in itself. Nothing is more certain to distort our motives or corrupt our cause. The applause of others can, like a caffeine rush, become addictive. Sugar-buzz spirituality is seductive but has no capacity to sustain.

The Bedroom

The lounge is the place where we are most often observed. The kitchen is where we feed. The bedroom reveals the source of our rest.

As we have just seen, if our success is measured by the accolades we receive from others then we may be due for some seriously disturbed and sleepless nights. Similarly, if numerical success is our sole criteria, spiritual insomnia is also not very far away.

Most pastors who have been in the ministry for any length of time will admit to a moment when they had considered resigning from their role. The reasons for resignation are many and varied. Tiredness, frustration, people pressure, domestic difficulties or financial constraints are just a few of the possible contributing factors.

I was just twenty-eight years of age when this possibility first occurred to me. I had come into the ministry young and had been put in charge of my first church shortly before my twenty-first birthday. I had stayed in that church for five years and was now three years into my second pastorate.

Ostensibly I was experiencing a measure of success – if success is to be measured only in numbers. The small church of fifty people had now grown to around eighty which my colleagues and friends told me was a healthy percentage increase. It also appeared that there was every indication the trend might well continue.

My problem was that church, as I saw it, was a million miles away from what I witnessed in the book of Acts. I concluded that, if we really were a Bible-believing community, the rate of growth should be exponentially more than it presently was and miracles should be a regular expression of grace within the life of the church.

As it was, one month three people might commit their lives to Christ and some time later perhaps two people might backslide. Miracles did happen in answer to prayer but there were a higher proportion of people that I prayed for, godly people at that, who remained in pain. As a young man I found it confusing and, though the reader my consider me naïve, this was an accurate reflection of how I was feeling at the time.

I considered the fact that a bricklayer might be faced with a pile of bricks as his day commenced and was able, as it concluded, to measure the height of the wall that he had built and leave with a sense of accomplishment for a job well done. Such luxury is usually denied the leader of the local church.

Added to this I was working extremely long hours. I looked for every possible opportunity to increase the size of the church. My patient congregation must have been sent dizzy by the launching of programme after programme. I jumped on every passing bandwagon in the hope that this would be the silver bullet – the ultimate elixir of spiritual life and growth.

I stood by the fire and gazed down at a chair to the left and said, 'Lord, I am going to write my letter of resignation to our denomination and nothing will dissuade me from doing it – short of an angelic visitation within the next few seconds.'

My father and grandfather had both been pastors and, while neither of them had gone out of their way to encourage me to enter the ministry, it crossed my mind that the step that I was about to take was likely to be something of a disappointment to them. I knew instinctively, however, they would support any decision that I considered to be the correct course of action.

As soon as I uttered the words the telephone rang. I was not expecting the caller to be an angel, but the person on the other end of the line was to prove to be the catalyst that was about to change the entire direction of my life.

Earlier that day I had visited a Christian bookshop to collect something that I had previously ordered and had now been told was in stock. The shop was run by a group of Christians who were considered by most local churches to be something less than kosher primarily because they were living in community and the structure of their meetings were unconventional. They also dressed like hippies at a time when most pastors, including myself, were never seen in public without a suit and tie.

I must have only been in the shop a matter of minutes. The transaction was simple and brief. I collected my book, paid and left. I would not have even been able to describe the young man that served me but, as I walked out (he later told me) he felt an incredible and overwhelming burden for the customer who had left – something that could not have been brought about by any signal of my demeanour. It was so intense that some time soon after he felt that he had to phone the leader of the small community – a man only slightly older than I was then, perhaps in his early thirties – to alert him.

It was this leader that was now on the phone. He related to me the account of the shop assistant and said that, as he prayed for me, the same burden came upon him. He went on to say that the Lord had told him to contact me immediately – hence the call.

Neither of us had met and the only way he was able to reach me was because the community had my contact details from when I had ordered the book. It was only because of this that he knew my name and learned that I was a pastor.

He suggested that I come round to see him as he said that he had a 'word' for me.

What happens next does not reflect well on me but, as I have written in a previous book that 'Hurt people hurt people and only whole people heal people' it is only fair to recount the story as it began to unfold. I was certainly hurting and was about to act in something less than grace.

I arrived back at the shop and was shown to a room above the premises. It was sparsely furnished with just a dilapidated table and a sofa that was so tired that the springs were clearly visible through it.

Standing opposite me was the 'elder'. His long hair and straggly beard fell across the shoulders of a crumpled T-shirt. Why, at a critical moment in my destiny, it occurred to me that it could do with a 'good iron' escapes me! But if nothing else it reveals how our priorities become blurred at such times and the inconsequential comes into focus, taking priority over what really matters.

It is the same kind of blindness that occurs when a meeting is in revival with people weeping and calling on God and one of the members notices that the communion table has been moved three metres and considers writing to the church leadership about it.

I stood in total contrast to the person across the shabby room. The immaculate suit and tie did well to disguise my crumpled spirit but for just a moment we looked at one another and were both aware of the incongruity of the situation. Here was a recently ordained minister of a respected denomination standing in front of someone who had never seen the inside of a Bible College and who looked like the lead singer of the Grateful Dead. Worst of all, for my struggling ego's sake, it was me looking for a word from God from him.

Almost immediately after I had entered the room and surveyed the scene he began to express the fact that he had prayed for me and began to bring me the revelation that he said God had for my life.

My arrogance did not allow him to continue and, even though I still had in mind the words I had uttered prior to his phone call I said, 'Hang on a moment, if you feel that you have got counsel for me don't you think it might be an idea to listen to the problem first . . .?'

Why lightning did not strike me from heaven at that moment I will never know, but the next words he said were to completely deflate my already bruised ego. 'John, you would have resigned earlier had not your father and grandfather been ministers and you were afraid of disappointing them.'

I sank into the sad sofa and felt the springs dig into me, creasing my pin-striped suit and further deflating my ego.

Words of knowledge really become signs and wonders at the point that they penetrate, laser-like, through the normally impervious barricades of bad attitude.

When he went on to tell me that God had told him to suggest a book that I should read, I desperately hoped, even despite my now chastened spirit, that it was not going to be the latest solution by an author who was convinced that he had discovered the last word on God's plan for the Church. I had already read too many of them and they had only served to demoralise me further.

To my surprise he spoke of a book written four hundred years ago written by a Puritan preacher called John Flavel. It was simply called *The Mystery of Providence*.[1]

The essence of what John Flavel wrote still proves pivotal in my ministry thirty years later – and more than 330 years after he wrote it. The lesson learned in that store room articulated principles and priorities that stay with me to this day. I had met an 'angel unawares'. He was not a supernatural entity but a flesh and blood brother who had listened to God and had the courage to communicate what he had heard.

The title of the book gave the message away. As I devoured page after page I learned that it was not my plans and programmes that built my church – in fact the church did not belong to me in the first place. Nor was it my ministry, personality or plans that was at the centre of the universe. God was.

I also leaned that when I went to sleep at night . . . God could actually cope without me. In short I learned what the providence and sovereignty of God really meant. He was the shepherd of the sheep, and whatever I would become or attain in the years that followed I was still, and would always be, an undershepherd.

A huge weight lifted from my shoulders. I had been released from a burden that I had never been called to carry. I had found my place of rest.

It is a rest that can only be found in an understanding of grace and sovereignty. It is a rest that totally relies on the endorsement of God rather than the approval of man. It is the rest reflected in the hymn by Keith Getty and Stuart Townend two verses of which say:

> IN CHRIST ALONE my hope is found,
> He is my light, my strength, my song;
> This Cornerstone, this solid Ground,
> Firm through the fiercest drought and storm.
> What heights of love, what depths of peace,
> When fears are stilled, when strivings cease!
> My Comforter, my All in All,
> Here in the love of Christ I stand.
>
> No guilt in life, no fear in death,
> This is the power of Christ in me;
> From life's first cry to final breath,

Jesus commands my destiny.
No power of hell, no scheme of man,
Can ever pluck me from His hand;
Till He returns or calls me home,
Here in the power of Christ I'll stand!
(Extract taken from 'In Christ Alone' Copyright (c) 2001
Thankyou Music)

The Bathroom

Within hours of the disciples' discussion about who was
the greatest among them, Jesus demolished their concept of the hierarchical pecking order by offering to
wash their feet.

Peter's reflex reaction was to immediately recoil from
such a suggestion but when Jesus said that were he to do
that he would have no part with him, he swung to the
other extreme by saying that in that case he would submit to a complete cleansing.

Jesus was quick to point out that only his feet needed
to be clean. Wearing, as was their custom, open sandals
it was not possible to travel any distance at all without
picking up the kind of grime that one might expect.

Nothing has changed. It is impossible for twenty-first
century disciples to travel any distance in a polluted
godless world without something from our surround-
ings clinging limpet-like to our spirit.

Those who have to work in a factory where expletives
and blasphemy hang like an audible wallpaper that
landscapes everyday life will know the impact of its
intrusive effect. This is one example of what happens in
a fallen world.

It is said that hundreds of metres underground in a
coalmine, workers may occasionally come across a small

white flower. Perhaps the seed has been transported from the surface on a miner's boot and somehow found a place to root. Even amid the darkness and the dust its petals remain a virgin white because something in its texture does not allow the dirt to cling.

In the world that you and I inhabit it is seldom as simple as that. Only regular examination of our spirit can ensure the hygiene of our hearts.

Dust in the Scriptures is often used as a spiritual metaphor for distress, poverty, unfruitfulness or sin. It is perhaps significant that the word appears in the story of Job more than in any other book of the Bible.

To be free from dust in the Scripture is to be free from poverty, poor self image and unfruitfulness. Two verses illustrate the point.

'He raises the poor from the dust and lifts the needy from the ash heap; he seats them with princes, with the princes of their people. He settles the barren woman in her home as a happy mother of children.'[2]

'He raises the poor from the dust and lifts the needy from the ash heap; he seats them with princes and has them inherit a throne of honour.'[3]

There are three primary expressions of this form of spiritual contamination. There is the dust that emanates out of the challenge of living in a fallen world and the circumstantial pain that accompanies it. There is the dust that arises out of the poor choices that we sometimes make – dust we bring upon ourselves. There is also the dust that can be dumped on us by others.

Though only one of the three categories are self-inflicted, in every case we have a responsibility to exercise cleansing. The presence of dust may not be our fault but the failure to cleanse it away can cause us to be culpable. To understand this we will need to look at the three areas in turn.

Circumstances

When blind Bartimaeus sat and begged all he ever asked for were a few coins to see him through to the next meal. With his beggar's cloak across his shoulders and a bowl to collect any charity that might be forthcoming, he sat in the same place each day in total dependence on those that ventured near and who might cast a few coins in his direction. Dust was his habitat. He lived in it. At the close of the day, before shuffling off to purchase his meagre rations, he would grope on the ground to see what had been left for him. Some of what was tossed towards him would have found the bowl but he would be sure to move his hands around to scoop up anything that lay to the side. In his poverty he could not afford to miss anything. By the time that he had finished he would probably have as much dust in his pockets as coins.

On the day that he heard that Jesus was in the area he rose to his feet and stumbled in the direction that he believed the sounds of the passing crowd were indicating. He clearly had faith that this day was going to be different because, as he rose, he dispensed with the beggar's cloak so that nothing would impede his progress. Everything about him indicated urgency and expectation – from pushing through the crowd when he eventually reached it, to shouting out to be heard by Jesus despite the calls on him from others to be quiet.

When Jesus called him forward the question he posed to Bartimaeus could have been perceived to be cruel. Why ask a blind man what he wanted? Perhaps because this man had lived all his life with the same poor plea pouring from his lips day after day – a cry for just enough income to see him through. But for Bartimaeus, dust and ash heaps were to no longer be a part of his destiny. He decided that day to go for gold when he replied, 'Lord, that I might receive my sight.'[4]

This man's experience of dust did not spring from any crime that he had committed or sins to which he had been seduced. He vacated his ash heap at the point that he decided that the presence of Jesus could be a passport to a new future. Like Gideon who climbed out of the pit with the limited strength that he had, so Bartimaeus jettisoned the trappings of confinement to run towards a future where he would not dwell in poverty and dust.

Personal Failure

When the Prodigal Son indicated that he wanted to leave home the message he gave was not only that he wanted the wealth that he considered due to him, but that he wanted it more than the presence of the father to whom it really belonged. What he was in effect saying was that, 'If I wait for your money until I inherit it on your death I may be too old to enjoy it. I choose it over you.' This is perhaps not a message to preach on Father's Day.

The Prodigal ran in precisely the opposite direction to Bartimaeus. The first ran from dust to cleansing. The second from the hygiene of the father's house to the putrefying stench and squalor of a pig pen. For a Jew to eat pork was reprehensible. To end up tending pigs was almost the lowest imaginable rung of the ladder. I say 'almost' for there was yet one step further into the dust. This man felt so low and desperate he considered eating the pig's food. Little wonder that when he approached the trough he concluded that enough was enough.

As he set off home to offer himself to his former household as a servant rather than a son, he carried only two things with him – grime on his garments and repentance in his heart. The former was the payment on his past, the wages of sin being death, and the latter was to be the pathway to his future.

Cleansing is inevitably linked to a change of direction married to a change of mind.

There are only two instances in the Scripture where we have a picture of God running. Jesus of course never ran because Jesus was never late.

In Song of Songs 2:8 we read of the bridegroom running towards the beauty of the bride. In the account of the Prodigal, we read of the father running towards the ugliness brought upon by the sin that had contaminated his son. That God should be drawn towards purity comes as no surprise. That he runs to those who return to him is a source of hope for all of us.

There are two Prodigals in the story. The son who remained at home was in his father's presence geographically but away from his father's heart emotionally. The evidence that the returning Prodigal, in contrast to the Prodigal Son who remained at home, was accepted was indicated by three gifts. The ring reminded him that he was still a son. The shoes showed that he had a future that was yet to be experienced. The cloak ensured that he no longer carried the censure associated with yesterday's failure. Dust was to be dispensed with – together with all the condemnation that came with it.

Cleansing in this context always costs something. Grace is free but that does not mean to receive it comes without any charge at all. The currency the prodigal used was not the coins he carried but the price he paid with his pride.

This principle of 'cost preceding cleansing' is seen in the account of the revival in Ephesus, an area riddled with sorcery and the occult.[5] Having heard the message and responded to it, those who had been involved in what we would call today New Age practices, returned urgently to their homes. Their objective was not to reflect on what they had heard but to act on it. They rooted out scrolls, parchments and anything that they could find connected with their past which they thought might be a stumbling block to their future growth. Having brought out all that they could find, they publicly burned them. The value is recorded and, in today's money, the conflagration would have cost over a million pounds sterling – approximately 1.7 million US dollars.

I preached on this passage a number of years ago and at the end of the service a businessman approached me and, with tears in his eyes, told me that within the next few days he would be dispensing with an area of his business that, though lucrative, he felt was incompatible with his testimony as a believer. I was to later learn that the decision involved tens of thousands of pounds. There is no doubt, however, that his long-term gain would have been incalculable.

On another occasion when speaking abroad, the local pastor indicated that two people wished to meet me at the end of the service before I left. The first told me that he had been making a great deal of money smuggling diamonds into the country. He said that, as a result of the message that morning, he had decided to stop and went on to say that he was now most likely to lose his home (which had a large mortgage dependent on the income from his lucrative trafficking). He now felt that he must be obedient to what God was saying to him, whatever the personal cost.

I prayed with him, aware that the second person was still patiently waiting in the wings. It transpired that the other person was the Chief of Police for the region who just wanted to greet me before he left the church!

Most people would not identify with a cleansing that involves crime but still have areas where spiritual hygiene needs to be addressed. It might involve dispensing with books or magazines. It may have to do with blocking certain TV channels or internet sites. It may even have to do with the cleansing of a hard drive on a computer.

When we read the Old Testament descriptions of the clothes of the High Priest in Leviticus 6:10 some might be forgiven for wondering about the twenty-first century relevance of such accounts. This might be especially true when details are provided about the nature of his underwear. It could possibly be that there might be something to be learned from the symbolism of outward adornment but why bother with vestments that cannot be seen? Why indeed? Perhaps these are areas of ministry, leadership and service that are the most important to God.

The imagery connected to the induction of the high priest is both powerful and poignant in this regard. As the robed priest came forward on the most important day of his life it would be easy for a sense of pride to rise in his spirit. He looked good and was the centre of everyone's attention. His appearance, however (and he would be aware of this), was about to be momentarily marred.

A bowl of blood was brought and applied to his right ear, his right thumb and his right toe.

Each of these areas were gateways: the ear to his mind; the thumb to his actions; and the toe to the direction that his ministry would take.

The concept of 'blood applied to gateways' reflects what happened at the first Passover. The angel of death was flying in judgement over the land. If the people of God wanted to prevent the death of their first-born they were instructed to apply blood to the lintel – the gateway of the house.

Cleansing comes at the point that all our gateways are similarly sanctified and protected. Cleansing is not about God 'keeping us in line' – it is about us taking responsibility for our personal health and well-being.

So far we have looked at the gateways that open towards us and from which we receive input. The tongue, however, is a gateway that expresses what is within us and has to be similarly guarded.

The book of James reminds us that the tongue can have an affirming and building capacity but also the potential to undermine and destroy. Gossip has the power to demolish reputations and inflict massive damage.

The word itself come from the old English *godsibb* which means 'godparent' or 'relating to God'. In days when much of the population could neither read nor write, and therefore could not record or journal, the *godsibb* had the important responsibility of passing on the oral stories and traditions within the family. One can imagine the power of such a person who, if they did not act with integrity, could rewrite history through the filter of their own personal prejudices.

It has been said that the gossip is a beast of prey that does not wait for the death of the creature that it devours[6] and also that we are always more willing to share the scoop about others than the scoop about ourselves.

Dust that is dumped upon us

As we have seen, there is dust that we carry that is a result of our circumstances and dust that pollutes us as a direct result of our personal choices. We are now going to look at how to deal with the dust that comes as a result of the negative actions of others around us.

When Jesus commissioned the disciples, and told them that they were to take the message of the kingdom from town to town, they began with a clean slate. Doubtless their emotions would have been mixed. It is likely that Thomas would have been worried and Peter, characteristically, impetuous. What they all had in common was that they had little knowledge of what lay ahead.

Jesus anticipated that there would be places where the message would be rejected and that they would be persecuted. To prepare them for such eventuality, he said 'And if any place will not welcome you or listen to you, shake the dust off your feet when you leave, as a testimony against them.'[7]

It is interesting to note that he did not speak about the message being rejected but about them being rejected. If they were stoned in the street, or had a hundred doors slammed in their faces, it was not the message that was going to take the flak, but their sense of well-being.

What most Christians would do today when faced with such rejection would be to give up in the place of supposed failure and move on to another town. At first glance it seems a sensible scenario. But there is a problem.

The clean slate that they started out with is no longer clean. When they enter the new town and knock on the first door, or start speaking in the public square, they are not starting in neutral as now their past experience is preparing their minds for further rejection. The fact is that every step of the journey from the town where they were hurt has been contaminated. They have carried something from the past that has the propensity to poison their future. It is like taking soil from Chernobyl and trying to grow good food in another location in the belief that a geographical move will make an inward change.

Jesus was acutely aware of the danger. The metaphor of the removal of dust from their feet was used to say, 'As you travel forward from the place of hurt do not take even the smallest particle of pain with you, for if you do, it will taint all your tomorrows.'

Bigger People do not despise the small things that can create havoc with the destiny that God has planned for them. It is so often the little foxes that spoil the vines.

On the physical level, there are few things more refreshing that a hot shower after a gruelling journey. It is just as true on a spiritual level:

> You who dwell in the dust, wake up and shout for joy. Your dew is like the dew of the morning; the earth will give birth to her dead.[8]

> So they shook the dust from their feet in protest against them and went to Iconium. And the disciples were filled with joy and with the Holy Spirit.[9]

The verse we alluded to earlier contrasted the dust-infested ash heap with a prince's throne and also drew a distinction between barrenness and fruitfulness. Isaiah proffers the same parallels:

> Awake, awake O Zion, clothe yourself with strength. Put on your garments of splendour . . . Shake off your dust; rise up, sit enthroned, O Jerusalem. Free yourself from the chains on your neck, O captive Daughter of Zion.[10]

It is as if the passage anticipates the parable of the Prodigal – a parable that would be related many hundreds of years later in its allusion to restored position, fruitfulness and fresh garments.

The Attic

Some years ago my wife and I returned from a time away from home to a house in total disarray – our lounge was drenched with water and the ceiling was bulging. It was clear that the problem had not begun on the ground floor so I raced to the bedroom above where I was faced with a similar situation. The bedroom was in the same sodden state and the ceiling ruined. The trouble had obviously originated in the attic where some plumbing had burst.

I learned a lesson that day that went far beyond the need to lag pipes in the winter. It was that anything that goes wrong in the attic will make its way eventually to the whole of the house. The place of rest was the first to be affected and eventually the place most accessible to others – the lounge.

From time to time we hear of internationally known leaders who fall. The phrase 'a scandal has come to light' is a telling one and usually indicates matters that may have been concealed for some considerable time.

When David repents of his adultery with Bathsheba, subsequent to having the laser light of prophecy shone into his 'attic' by Nathan, he comes to the conclusion, 'Surely you desire truth in the inner parts; you teach me wisdom in the inmost place.'[11]

In our present house we have never ventured into the attic as it is too shallow to be functional. In a previous home the area was suitable for conversion into a room. Usually, when doing a loft conversion, the first thing to be installed in the attic is electricity. This is simply because illumination is needed before cleaning and cannot be effectively done without it.

There is what we might call a 'spiritual physics' that demands that everything at the top tends to flow downwards. We understand such gravitational pulls in the natural realm but sometimes tend to ignore them in the economy of the kingdom of God. In the following passage note the directional words such as 'down' and 'descending':

> Behold, how good and how pleasant it is for brethren to dwell together in unity! It is like the precious oil upon the head, running down on the beard, the beard of Aaron, running down on the edge of his garments. It is like the dew of Hermon, descending upon the mountains of Zion; for there the LORD commanded the blessing—Life forevermore.[12]

That God commands blessing is a wonderful concept as is the fact that 'Brethren dwell together in unity.' However, the directional flow of unity, and subsequently, refreshing is pivotal.

A church leadership who model wholesome authentic relationship will have an exponential effect on the life of the local church that goes far beyond sermons preached and teachings taught.

In one church I pastored one of my elders asked if he could make an appointment to meet me regarding what he believed to be a serious matter. Shortly into the interview he indicated that he wished to resign his position and step down from office. He went on to say that he could not escape the fact that the Bible required those in his position to be 'apt to teach' and, as this was not a gift he possessed, came to the conclusion that he did not meet the requisite criteria. Certainly all the other elders were gifted communicators and Bible teachers. Did this then mean he was unqualified?

The elder concerned also served as our treasurer. There were times when large financial projects were inaugurated that he faced penetrating questions in church meetings and, on every occasion, he did so with a gracious and patient spirit. I went on to tell him that if I wanted to give an example of innate godliness to someone in the church who had recently come to faith – it is more than likely that his name would come to mind. He teaching was not articulated in alliterative sermon outlines. His was the hermeneutic of a life that operated as a working model of what was believed. I was able to convince him that he should not only retain his role as an elder, but that he was one of the most effective teachers in the church. I was aware that because he was a leader, his character and disposition was very likely to flow into the wider body of the church.

Of course, the antithesis is also true. Parents whose relationship is characterised by constant arguing, and regular rows are inevitably going to pass something 'down' to their children that may later be manifested in emotional insecurity and an inadequate sense of how family should work.

What lives in the innermost part of our spirit will eventually seep through to our public persona.

The word 'hypocrite' carries with it a sense of speaking from behind a mask. The function of a mask is to present an image in public which is not a true representation of the face hidden behind it.

On one occasion when Jesus was teaching on the subject he chose to use the metaphor of the house:

> Beware of the leaven of the Pharisees, which is hypocrisy. For there is nothing covered that will not be revealed, nor hidden that will not be known. Therefore whatever you have spoken in the dark will be heard in the light, and what you have spoken in the ear in inner rooms will be proclaimed on the housetops.[13]

That is why living in a sense of regular and transparent repentance is required if we want to operate in the rest and security that God desires for us.

A graphic illustration of what life is like outside those perimeters is found in Proverbs when the person who hoards in the attic that which he hopes will not be revealed: and subsequently lives in perpetual tension.

'The wicked man flees though no-one pursues, but the righteous are as bold as a lion.'[14]

Another form of hypocrisy is the cosmetic surgery of spin.

Image-conscious celebrities would not dream of having their picture appear on the front cover of a glossy magazine that had not been, in their view, properly processed. However beautiful the model might be, the merest mention of a blemish cannot be countenanced. There is regular evidence in the media of publishers who go much further than that; where figures are slimmed down or expanded in a way that can only be described as post-production surgery. It does not hurt a bit because the source is never altered. Fiction is more palatable than fact in a world where perception is deemed more acceptable than reality.

Before an artist, traditional or digital, addresses their subject in paint or pixels they are aware of what is called 'Divine Proportion' – something recognised throughout history as an outline most pleasing to the eye. Mathematically it is a ratio of 1:1.61803398874989. How the formula was discovered remains a mystery but it has been used by artists, architects and designers from the days of Michelangelo.

People started prioritising presentation over truth right at the beginning of history. It commenced the moment that Adam and Eve sewed fig leaves to cover the consequence of their sin, in order to appear differently to God than they really were.

The engagement of spin rather than the confession of sin is a strand to be found woven throughout the entire fabric of biblical revelation. The texture of the thread is seen in the text that tells of a heart that is 'deceitful above all things and beyond cure.'[15]

One of the many arguments for the authenticity of the Bible is that there is no agenda, with those who wrote under divine inspiration, to airbrush out the faults and foibles of the characters – even the ones deemed to be 'spiritual'. It does not gloss over, for example, Noah's drunkenness, David's adultery or Moses' trouble with his temper.

Jesus is returning for a bride 'without stain or wrinkle'[16] but this will be the process of a growth that arises out of grace, not the artistry of an airbrush.

The two principle squatters that endeavour to steal a place in our lofts are linked by the single word 'fear'. The first is related to sin and the second to inadequacy. In the first it is the fear of being found out and in the second, the fear of not living up to standard that we have set for ourselves or someone else has put in place for us.

Big People have to be big enough to deal with both these intrusive spectres.

Fear is something that we all have to face and cannot be completely escaped from. Not only is it common to everyone but, in some cases, is necessary for the safety and security of our lives. Children, for instance, need to understand from an early age a necessary fear of fire, traffic and of talking to strangers.

However, when fear begins to dominate the core of who we are then its effects become pernicious: undermining our personality and potentially wrecking our hopes and dreams.

Fear (False Evidence Appearing Real) robs tomorrow of its blessing and today of its strength. If its natural habitat is the darkness of our attic then it will most certainly creep like an assassin to destroy every sense of rest and peace.

Whole books have been dedicated to the issue and it is not my purpose to develop the subject at any length here. However, it is important for the Christian, more than anyone else, to understand that fear is based upon a lie. It feeds upon a lie and is kept alive by a lie. The lie is that God is not sovereign and in control, and that we are the victims of random factors in a meaningless universe. However, God is on the throne and he has promised us that no weapon formed against us will prosper.

On one occasion a well-known Christian leader was staying in our home. We had not spent quality time together for many months and so remained talking well into the night. Before we eventually retired to bed the conversation had, for whatever reason, ventured into the area of demon possession and that was what was on our minds as we went off to our rooms.

When we have friends staying with us it is normal for us to leave a light on on the landing so that they can easily make their way around the house if necessary during the night.

At the breakfast table the next day my friend asked if my wife and I were aware of his screams as we slept, as he was worried he had woken us. We assured him we had not been disturbed but obviously wanted to know what had happened. He related to us his story.

In the early hours of the morning, while it was still dark, he became aware of a presence in the room and confessed that he was too terrified to even open his eyes. To his horror he came to the realisation that the spectre had taken on a physical manifestation and had begun moving from the foot of the bed, along his body and towards his throat. Too petrified to move a muscle or open his eyes lest what would appear before him was too terrifying, he commenced praying out loud and calling upon every formulae for deliverance that his addled mind could muster. Nothing worked and the pressure around his neck was continued. He continued to call on the Lord convinced that he was in mortal danger.

He realised that as a Christian, not least a notable Christian leader, it surely behoved him to at least open his eyes. He must, he finally resolved, command the demon to leave. Slowly opening his eyes he let out a frantic scream. In the darkness silhouetted by the landing light was what appeared to be a horned head ominously framing slanting eyes.

It was at that moment that a scream that mirrored his own rent the room – as our Siamese cat leapt in terror from his bed!

What had happened was that the cat, unused to anyone being in the spare room, through curiosity had climbed onto the bed. She had proceeded to walk up his body towards his head. What was in her mind – as with a paw on each of his shoulders, she stood silently looking down onto a tortured face that interceded for deliverance and quoted sacred texts – is only a matter for conjecture.

We laughed about the story the following day, and I hope that you enjoyed it too, but we also learned the lesson that it is not only children who fret about spectres at the window that turn out to be no more than the swaying branches of a tree. The children of God can be similarly disturbed by the lie of the enemy that suggests that we are abandoned, powerless, loved less than we are or alone.

6

Space for Grace

One of the primary reasons for what we call 'unanswered prayer' is that we sometimes see intercession as having two dimensions rather than three. The normal concept is that, assuming God's willingness and the timing being right, all we have to do is to link our need to God's supply and the subsequent answer will fall neatly into our lap. However, the third element, which I have termed 'space for grace' must also be in place. Let me explain.

Some time ago my wife and I were watching a news report about the A380 Airbus – the largest passenger aircraft in the world. It can carry 550 passengers and fly ten thousand miles without refuelling and was about to land at one of London's main airports for the first time. The announcer, perhaps misreading her autocue, said, 'And shortly the A380 Airbus will be flying into Heathrow to see if the landing strip is big enough . . .' Not a good idea!

Let's take a step back and look at the scenario. The first thing that we are aware of is that all airports would like to receive the A380 as this brings necessary revenue to their cities. The second factor is that the airline that owns the A380 needs to be able to land somewhere. Clearly, if they cannot land then all the millions spent in development will be wasted and no future income can be accrued to offset their investment.

Immediately we recognise the difficulty. The issue is not linking the need on earth (the airport) to the desire in the heavens (the airline). It is the length of the runway that is available to receive what heaven wants to bring – and this brings with it a high degree of cost. At the time of writing Los Angeles airport has set aside fifty million dollars: not to purchase another plane or build another terminal but just to make a runway large enough to take the A380.

Put another way, you have got to make space on earth for anything big you are expecting from heaven.

Let's push the metaphor a little further. That a suburban airport will not receive the new aircraft has nothing to do with sin in their life or an innate stubbornness in the airline authorities. It is simply an issue of available landing strip. Small runways are forever destined to receive light aircraft and big airports are going accept jumbo jets.

Bigger People understand this clearly. They know exactly what Jesus meant when he said, 'According to your faith will it be done to you'.[1]

Small airports can pray until their knees are raw and fast until they are skeletal. They will only get large aircraft at the point that they make space for what, in many cases, is already waiting for them in heaven because it simply cannot land.

As I write, the National Leadership Team and myself have put in place, with the backing of our conference, the construction of a new international centre for our denomination in the heart of the UK at a cost of 12 million pounds This is not only a reflection of what we need now: it is a statement about how we are trusting in God for the future – a future that will extend long beyond my tenure as General Superintendent into the generations that are to come.

We are going to look at the outworking of this 'space for grace' principle by looking at four examples from the life of Elisha.

Space for Grace in Our Spirit

The background to 2 Kings 3 is a devastating national drought. The absence of rain was so serious that three kings, the politicians of the day, were in desperate need for a word from God and so set out in search of a prophet. What a different world we would see today if all politicians made an understanding of the will of God their priority.

The problem in this instance, as we are about to see, was not with the politicians but with the prophet himself.

The initial problem for Elisha was not that he had a 'small airstrip' because he was clearly a man of faith. When Elijah, whom he has served, was caught up in a fiery chariot to heaven, Elisha requested a double portion of his anointing. That certainly was a huge runway to build and, if we count the number of miracles that took happened throughout his ministry, we discover that double the number of Elijah's recorded miracles took place.

It was not that Elisha did not have an airstrip; it was that his runway had rubble on it. Consequently, what was hovering in heaven had to be held in a holding pattern until the required space could be cleared.

The nation needed revelation urgently. There was already a need on earth and willingness in heaven but, as we have already seen, those two factors alone were insufficient to bring into place the fruits of intercession.

Another factor needs to be understood in order to grasp how dire this situation had become. If God wants to speak to your city, and your church is not in a place spiritually to hear what God is saying, then he will speak through another leadership and another church. In our society there are many thousands of people who are capable of hearing, and subsequently bringing, a word from the Lord.

In the context of the passage we are about to consider, though there were other prophets, it was Elisha who was specifically sought out as he was a nationally known figure. Because he previously was known to have the ear of God, it followed that he would also have the ear of kings.

It would seem, however, that Elisha harboured something in his spirit. This meant that even though God wanted to land with revelation, the runway was not vacant. God refused to do so in the same way that doves, however hungry, refuse to descend on road kill.

It is sobering to note that God makes no exceptions for his cardinal principals. It mattered not that Elisha had performed miracles in the past, nor that he had religious status. It was not his track record yesterday that was important to God, it was the impediment that was on his track today that was the problem. We alluded to this previously when we considered the issue of Moses and circumcision and the danger of exceptionalism. But let's read the account for ourselves:

> But Jehoshaphat asked, "Is there no prophet of the LORD here, that we may enquire of the LORD through him?"
> An officer of the king of Israel answered, "Elisha son of Shaphat is here. He used to pour water on the hands of Elijah."
> Jehoshaphat said, "The word of the LORD is with him." So the king of Israel and Jehoshaphat and the king of Edom went down to him.

Elisha said to the king of Israel, "What do we have to do with each other? Go to the prophets of your father and the prophets of your mother."

"No," the king of Israel answered, "because it was the Lord who called us three kings together to hand us over to Moab."

Elisha said, "As surely as the Lord Almighty lives, whom I serve, if I did not have respect for the presence of Jehoshaphat king of Judah, I would not look at you or even notice you.[2]

As I read I see a prophet with an attitude problem. The good news appears to be that, as he was speaking, he became aware of this himself.

Some commentators may say that his response was legitimate but what he did next offers a clue to his need to step back, to quieten his spirit and to recalibrate his responses.

He called for a harpist, of all things.

Let me say at this point that the musicians in our churches, whatever tradition we are part of, are not the supporting cast for the preacher. Much less are they there to fill in the first forty-five minutes until the main event. They have a ministry in their own right. On many occasions I have felt that I been spoken to by God through the music as much as I have through the preached word.

Now I know that, as soon as I say this, the hackles in some may be raised. This may well be because of a proclivity in a minority of musicians, artistic temperament being what it is, to 'take the service over'. Or for those in the congregation to say, 'The presence of God was so real in the meeting that we didn't have time for the word.'

Of course, preaching, in whatever form it takes, must be central and there are times when we must happily allow for whatever God might want to do in a service. But this does not take away from the recognition of music as a ministry with the potential to speak into the lives of the worshipper as well as lead them closer to God in devotion.

What we do know is that when the harpist played something happened in Elisha's spirit. And when something happens in us something often also happens in the heavenlies. The hand of God that had been held in a holding pattern was now given clearance to land.

'While the harpist was playing, the hand of the LORD came upon Elisha.'[3]

Someone might ask who on earth has the ability to give God clearance for anything? They may have also asked that after learning of the time in the gospels when Jesus *was unable to do any mighty work* in one town *because of their unbelief.*

Once again we notice that it is not a matter of need in the town or willingness in the heavens: there has to be a large enough landing strip. There has to be sufficient faith to receive it. Yet another instance of a city that needed a jumbo jet but which only gave clearance for light aircraft.

Elisha was learning a lesson that was, as we shall see later, pivotal to his future ministry. More importantly we have seen that spiritual enlargement, the growth into Bigger People, is not the sole prerogative of the new convert. People can be long in service but shallow in spirituality. It is depth of commitment that God looks for, as well as length.

Nor does size or presence preclude the possibility that those who were giants at one period in their lives, can descend to living their lives as dwarfs.

When Saul, who was head and shoulders taller than anyone in Israel, was missing at his own coronation he was not detained on a matter of supreme national importance. Rather, the giant was cowering on the ground behind stacks of packing cases and baggage on the perimeter of the camp. He was terrified of being unequal to the responsibility and so, like the man who was later to hide his talent in ground, nervously shrank away into the shadows.

God is looking for Bigger People. Not just big names with established credentials but those who will step up to the plate and stand in God's strength.

Space for Grace in Our Circumstances

We are about to see two illustrations of this: one national and one personal.

National

When God brought the revelation to Elisha it was to have powerful repercussions. The 'space for grace' principle was once again going to be applied. The command that came, subsequent to his runway being cleared, was to dig ditches throughout the entire valley areas.

The need on earth and the willingness of heaven had now been established but God will not waste blessing.

We considered earlier the danger of gully-washer blessing that only touches our lives superficially. Yet the digging of the ditch is not just about the retention of blessing but also about the space that we give to God in order to be used by him in service.

All preachers use illustrations and most will have stories that mean a lot to them and which will regularly arise in their mind, whether they choose to use them or not. One such favourite with me is the story of an elderly lady, well into her eighties, who lived in the Republic of Ireland.

For those reading this and who are not familiar with the geography of Ireland I should mention that the Republic is a beautiful and largely rural country that, until recent years, has had comparatively few evangelical churches.

The lady in our story lived in a small village many miles away from her church but, happily, there was a young man who lived even further away who would drive past her home and take her to the services she anticipated so keenly.

All went well until he moved away and it appeared that this lady would never have fellowship again in her remaining years. It was impracticable for the church to pick her up and return her home each Sunday as the distance was so great. At first she seemed resigned to her fate.

It was then she thought of an idea. She would visit everyone in her village and ask them if they would like to join her on a Sunday morning for a Bible reading and a time of prayer in her small cottage. She was not a preacher but opening her home would not be beyond her; especially if she could find other people in a situation similar to her own.

The first person that she asked was her neighbour. She related her story and her plan but her friend declined saying that she hoped all went well but the arrangement was not really for her.

Undeterred she set about calling on more homes. Initially she visited her friends and acquaintances but, as her confidence grew, she also knocked the doors of people who were previously unknown to her. A few weeks later her neighbour asked how the meetings were going as she had noticed people calling at the cottage from time to time. 'Oh, it is wonderful,' said the elderly lady, 'last Sunday we had eight people in the front room and the room was full.'

Some time later the same person asked the same question which elicited almost the same response except she was told, 'We had twelve people in the front room and the front room was full.' And then, a month or two later, 'We had fifteen people and the front room was full.'

Somewhat disconcerted the neighbour asked if they were talking about the same room – or perhaps she had built an extension.

'Oh no,' responded the elderly lady, 'It is exactly the same room that was full on the first occasion. However, I then wondered what we would do the following week if anyone else turned up. I noticed a sideboard with some lovely ornaments on it and realised that, if I could have that moved to another room, it would create space for at least three chairs. I had more furniture moved each time I faced the same difficulty. I was correct in saying the room was full when it held eight and I was correct when I said the room was full when it held fifteen. It is the same room, it is just that I prioritised what it was "full of" in order to make more room for what I believed God wanted to do.'

What a story! You probably realise now why I love it so much.

The first point at which this lady 'made space for grace' was when she realised that her age did not matter. She was not going to listen to the devil's lie that her time was over. The second enlargement of her runway occurred at the point that, having visited the people she knew, she summoned the courage to call on those who had previously been unknown to her. The third place she made space was in her home. The furniture's removal and the reprioritising of the legitimate space it had occupied was the equivalent of digging one of Elisha's ditches.

We often conclude that God only wants us to move from our lives those things that are wrong. The fact is that the most important stage of growth in those who yearn to be Bigger People is when they re-prioritise legitimate things and relegate them to lower position of importance in order that God's purposes can be better served.

The Amplified Bible says:

> Everything is permissible (allowable and lawful) for me; but not all things are helpful (good for me to do, expedient and profitable when considered with other things). Everything is lawful for me, but I will not become the slave of anything or be brought under its power.[4]

There is a sense in which it would be possible to double the effective size of a church without adding a single new member. That is exactly what would take place if each of us could doubled the effective space that we are currently making available to God.

This is what we mean by the Lordship of Christ: the bringing of every part of our lives under his rule and authority.

When I was a young man I was invited to hear an American Bible teacher and he took this subject as his topic. At the conclusion of the message he told the congregation that he was not going to conduct the normal type of appeal as he felt that, if he were to ask those listening to raise their hands to indicate if they believed Jesus was Lord of their lives, it was likely that everyone would respond.

Instead he said he would ask everyone to close their eyes and visualise their house and then imagine God reaching down and taking it away. As everyone remained in an attitude of prayer he said that only if we were in a state of peace as we considered this eventuality, could Jesus be considered Lord.

I was in a great state of peace – primarily because I did not own a house.

The next step was to imagine the same thing with our cars. I must confess to feeling a twinge of regret as I pictured mine being whisked away but, as it was nothing too acute, I concluded that Jesus must therefore be Lord also as far as I was concerned.

The service over, we eventually made our way out of the church building to go home. I strode over to where I had parked my car and all I saw was a vacant space. It had been stolen. I got it back some days later, and of course God was not culpable in the felony – but it did give me cause to consider how lightly we refer to lordship both in the words that we say and the worship songs that we sing.

The disciples may well have thought that Jesus was implicating them in vehicle theft in the story we recall on Palm Sunday.

When transportation is needed to enter Jerusalem, the Lord instructs his disciples to fetch a donkey tethered outside a man's house. He furnishes them with the donkey's location and points out that the owner had never ridden it himself as yet. We sometimes get so taken up with the picture of palm branches and cheering crowds calling 'hosanna', that we miss the account that precedes that part of the narrative.

Imagine for a moment that Jesus had told us that he needed transport and that around a corner we would find a newly registered vehicle just delivered from the dealership. Additional information includes the fact that the doors are open and the keys are in the ignition. We are then told not to worry if we are challenged for, if anyone should question the act, all that we needed to say was that 'The Lord needed it' and they would be certain to release it to us.

Both Mark and John relate that when they were untying the colt, and were subsequently challenged, the key phrase 'The Lord needs it'[5] was all that was necessary to put the mode of transport under their control.

We have no idea who the owners were as their names are not mentioned. It would be purely conjecture to conclude that, after God's intervention in their life, they offered all of their other possessions too, if Jesus should require them.

What we can be totally sure of is that Jesus would not take anything that had not been first submitted to him. We are also confident in the fact that the owners knew that 'Lord' was not just a title of honour or respect. It represented a commitment that was total and unreserved.

It is not donkeys that we have to untie in our culture but vehicles of another nature. They are the means that can be used to transport the will of God to the places that he needs to reach.

Any who argue that they cannot currently submit their finances to God on the basis that their money is 'all tied up at the moment', may need to hear the words, 'Untie it and let it go, the Lord needs it.'

The same may need to be said to those who cannot serve because, as far as time is concerned, they are 'all tied up at the moment'. And what shall we say of those who recoil from sharing their faith with family or friends because they are concerned about getting tongue-tied?

Of course, the idea that God needs anything in the first place is a difficult concept to grasp for some of us. But that is how God has ordered his world. He could have used angels, and sometimes does, but he mainly chooses to use you and me – remarkable though that may seem.

Using the word 'Lord', as we so often do, is in fact to say that we are creating the ultimate space in our lives for God. Nothing can be left unsurrendered, nothing held back and nothing given a higher priority than compliance to whatever call he might make upon our lives.

Prayer is not about asking God to endorse our agendas. It entails a willingness to discover God's mind on a matter, and putting everything that we posses at his disposal.

Personal

Although we have already applied the national illustration of the reversal of the drought to a personal level, the next section pertains to a very individual need indeed. The account that follows a dearth of water, now deals with a lack of oil – interestingly both being symbols of the Holy Spirit. Though each story physically happened in time and space to real people, the spiritual parallels should not be missed.

Elisha now encounters a distraught woman at the lowest point in her life.

When Elijah had been under the juniper tree telling God that he felt that he was about the only believer left, he was reminded that there were 7,000 that had not bowed the knee to Baal. It was likely that this woman's husband, now deceased, was one of them.

When a woman was widowed in that culture and she was alone, her own demise was virtually guaranteed. In this case the woman had two sons but the debt with which she had been left was so great that, having nothing of value left in the house, the bailiffs were on their way to take her boys as slaves in lieu of the money that could not be raised.

When Elisha asks what she has in the house she tells him that she has nothing except a little oil.

In an earlier chapter we looked at her life with regard to the empty vessels that she was required to bring. Now we are to look at the miracle in a different context.

Within a short space of time this lady's life is about to be totally transformed from littleness to largeness and from confinement to plenty. The way that this happens is much more than the interesting details of a captivating tale. In the account there are a number of primary principles that are as pertinent to receiving provision in the twenty-first century as ever they were in her day.

What doesn't happen is the prophet taking her small jar of oil, praying over it, and seeing it miraculously filled to the brim. This may seen too obvious a point to mention until we realise that is precisely what we expect when we come to God with our own sense of emptiness.

We tell him that we are not feeling fulfilled (filled full) in our church, our ministry, our finances or our family. It seems logical therefore to conclude that the answer to emptiness is fullness.

What we are now about to discover is one of the most pivotal factors in the whole theme of becoming Bigger People.

The answer to emptiness is not more fullness it is more emptiness.

Elisha responds to her need by requiring that she exponentially multiplies her emptiness by asking all her neighbours for as many empty vessels as she can muster.

Earlier in this chapter we noticed that God does not waste blessing as huge ditches had to be dug to contain the needed water. The answer to emptiness was not fullness but more emptiness. The same scenario is now taking place with the oil.

When the woman obediently brought the empty vessel back to the house (and obedience is always the precursor of a miracle) we find that a few others remarkable principles are about to be put into practice.

When I heard this story as a boy in Sunday school I always assumed that she brought the vessels back to Elisha who subsequently performed the miracle. After all she was just a poor widow and he was a powerful man of God. It did not happen like that at all.

The prophet was not even there when the miracle took place. At his instruction she and her sons locked themselves in the house. We have to remember that the creditors could call at any time. There is usually a gap between the promise of a miracle and the provision of a miracle. It is vital that we lock the door on the devil's lie that says that delay is denial. The devil had robbed her of her past (her husband) – she must not now be robbed of her future (her sons).

The prophet did not need to be there. She had made space for grace and now God was going to grant her enlargement based on her own faith and obedience.

When her sons brought her the last vessel the oil stopped flowing and the miracle ceased. When there was no more space there was no more miracle.

Let's imagine what God could have done. He could have looked at the half-empty jar that she had begun with and sent a deluge of oil that filled the vessel, flowed over the floor of the kitchen, out of the house and into the town. Millions of litres of oil supplied and millions wasted. The provision alone would not make the woman a penny richer.

If I were to ask a three-year-old child to fill me a cup of water from the tap she would turn off the supply when the cup was almost full. No more cup – no more water.

I am aware that my books are read by a wide cross-section of Christians from seasoned leaders to those who have only recently come to faith. The following illustrations will highlight how the 'space for grace' principle might be applied in specific situations.

- Samantha has not been a Christian for very long. She has a friend at her office that really needs prayer. She thinks of Joan – someone who has been a believer considerably longer than she has. Perhaps she will introduce her friend to Joan. If we were to suggest to Samantha that she prays for her friend herself she may retort that she could never do that. All she really means is that she has never done that before. There is a space in her experience that has never been occupied by action. Asking Joan might meet her friend's need but it would not make a bigger person of Samantha. At the point she decides that she will pray, she has brought an area of emptiness to God. Every space we give to God he will fill. As she does this she is enlarged. The answer now is not to rest on her laurels but to think of other things that she has been previously reticent to do. Remember – no more cup – no more water.

- Joan has been a Christian for a while now and is happy to pray with people but as yet has never attempted to lead anyone to Christ. Steve is her cousin and he has been asking a lot of questions recently. Perhaps if she could get Steve to meet her pastor . . . Of course, there is no doubt that the pastor would be delighted to talk to Steve but there are a couple of issues. The first is that Steve knows his cousin but has never met the pastor. Another is that Joan is there now

and the minister is not. Why create more hurdles?
Joan decides that she is now going to make space for
God to use her and attempt to lead her cousin to faith.

Faith is not believing that 'God can do it.' The devil has
that kind of faith. The fact is that, in that area, he has
probably more faith than the Church. That is why he
spends so much of his energy ensuring that the Church
is confined.

He is far more aware of what might happen were the
Church to wake up to what God could do through it
than the Church is. Dare we suggest that one of the reasons why the enemy does not incite the authorities to
throw Christians into prison in the west is that we have
already chosen to lock ourselves inside the local church
and have thrown away the key?

Faith is not just believing that God can do it, it is only
real faith when we believe that God can do it through us.
For Samantha to take her friend to Joan expresses that
she has faith – but it is more in Joan than in God.
Similarly, for Joan to introduce Steve to the pastor
implies she has more faith in the pastor than she does in
God.

• The pastor is leading a growing church. With people
  like Samantha and Joan in it, it is hardly surprising. It
  is his good teaching that is releasing people to mature
  in what they understand about faith and how faith
  can be can applied. He is not enslaved to statistics. But
  because he has sought to build Bigger People rather
  than just bigger numbers God, as so often is the case,
  has given him the numbers as well.

  The morning service has reached 80 per cent of the
  capacity of the building. Church growth consultants
  have long been aware that when a congregation fills

85 per cent of the capacity of the building growth usually stalls. The reason is simple. Most people want to sit where they want to sit. If week after week their family cannot sit together they reluctantly may vote with their feet and find another church. This is not rocket science and the wisdom of the consultant is hardly necessary. The three-year-old girl has already worked it out – no more cup, no more water.

The minister has several options: relocate to new premises, rebuild on the current site or hold multiple services. All of them come with a challenge. Some people may leave if he relocates. If the church changes to multiple services the feeling of a less than half-full building may totally change the ambience of the worship service. However, if action is not taken growth will stall. Numbers may eventually decline if it is perceived that the leadership is unable to address such an obvious need.

- The elders are thrilled at the progress of the church. They are willing to support their minister in his vision to go to multiple services as a first stage, on the understanding that relocation will eventually be necessary. There is, however, a further difficulty. Their minister is working very long hours and it is evident that he has been cutting back on necessary family time. Expanding opportunities for the church has not been paralleled with the provision of extra hours in the day. It is clear that the pastor needs additional staff. But can they opt for the additional cost of a ministry team when they may be soon facing the expenditure of a new building? Space in a church context is spiritual, physical, emotional and material.
- The congregation is excited about what is happening in their church – at least most of them are. Some who were present when the church was small can hardly

believe what God is doing among them. They are growing larger in numbers, deeper in fellowship and wider in influence. Big People rejoice when they see growth in any way it manifests itself. However, not everyone is happy. A tiny minority have realised something about growth that is unpalatable. They may not articulate it in the formulae that follows but the essence of their complaint is expressed by it. When they only had fifty members they had 2 per cent of the minister's attention. Now it's four hundred and they are concerned that their visibility, perhaps even importance has been reduced to 0.25 per cent. What, they anxiously ask themselves, would happen if the congregation grew to a thousand? But surely God would not let a terrible thing like that take place.

The above illustrations show that the 'space for grace' principle – permeates every area of the church.

The Mind

Few things inhibit growth more than an unhelpful culture – the mindset of the church. The minister and the elders must address the issue with some urgency before they can expect the fellowship to move to the next stage in its development.

Steve has now joined the church and does not only recognise a different culture; he thinks he is on a different planet – almost a parallel universe. Much of what he is experiencing is good. He now realises that previously he was only two-thirds alive. He has always had a body and has been able to communicate with the physical world around him. He has also had a soul and this part of his personality has been his stairway to relationships and to music, art and literature. He had of course been previously dead to God. Now he is born again and is spiritually alive. The Bible is no longer a book he can read; but a book that reads him. Prayer, if he ever used it, was employed like the spare wheel in the car – vital in a crisis but ignored outside of one. Now he is talking to God and he is hearing God speak it all the various ways that God loves to communicate. He literally is a new man.

Steve, however, has a problem. It's not something that is going to shake his faith but it troubles him nevertheless.

Steve is a young and successful businessman in the city. He knows that few things are achieved without investment but wonders if that is part of the mindset of his church. In the secular world of which he is a part, his company invest in him attending conferences that will increase his skill base and stretch his thinking. From where stands, he does not see ongoing training as a priority for the leadership of the church. It appears to him that his pastor is overstretched and the leadership around him seem unaware of the need to give their minister space to develop. It's almost as if the pastor is a man struggling to cut down a tree but is too busy to sharpen his axe.

This highlights the fact that the principles we are considering are sometimes seen sooner by the secular world than by the Church. Jesus talked in parables because he knew that all truth was parallel. Invest your seed to reap a harvest, invest your capital to gain a profit.

Little wonder that Jesus said, 'the people of this world are more shrewd in dealing with their own kind than are the people of the light.'[6]

It's now time to get back to Elisha and we find him within hours of his death.[7]

Into his bedroom comes the king of Israel in great distress. The two men could hardly be more different. One is politically powerful, physically strong, politically astute and emotionally insecure with his whole life in front of him. Elisha, on the other hand, is spiritually powerful, physically weak, emotionally secure and about to die.

The king is weeping not just because a great spiritual leader is dying but, as the text illustrates, out of a desperate fear for what will happen to the nation when Elisha has gone.

I wonder if I – as a preacher – became aware that I was shortly to die, and only had one final message to bring, which I would choose. It would be sure to be a theme that had been fundamental to my understanding of the purposes of God and epitomised the most important facet of my personal vision and values.

For Elisha there was no contest. However, this would not turn out to be a formal sermon, and in many ways he wished it was not necessary to preach it, but 'space for grace' was what he decided to communicate at that important moment.

He had realised the truth of it when he had decided to clear the runway of the rubble of a poor attitude. This was when he was waiting to hear God's revelation for the nation. When he later had instructed that ditches should be dug to contain God's provision the sermon was reiterated again. When he encouraged the poor widow to increase her emptiness to receive the necessary fullness that God had for her, the same sentiments were expressed.

Now he is faced, not with the weakest woman in society, but the most powerful man. The principles, however, remain exactly the same.

Elisha directs Jehoash to a bow and a cluster of arrows and asks him to bring the bow and one of the arrows to the window with the instruction that he should shoot towards the the Arameans, his potential enemy.

It was very clear that the king was lacking faith for the prophet felt the need to extend his own feeble hands and place them over the hands of Jehoash with a view to him pulling the string of the bow further back. This was yet another example of making space for grace and encouraging him to think more expansively. When the string was at full stretch the king released the arrow and Elisha declared that this was symbolic of the victory he would have.

A problem still remained, however. How much of the trajectory of the arrow was a result of the king's faith and how much came from the faith of the prophet? Elisha had to be sure.

He then asked Jehoash to grasp the remaining arrows and bang them on the ground. This time Elisha did not extend his hand or offer his help. It was the same scenario as when he had decided to leave the widow and her sons to be the catalysts of their own miracle.

We have to learn that while prophets are not always around – God is.

The king did as he was instructed and feebly tapped the bundle on the ground but then stopped. Frail or not, Elisha became angry and shouted at Jehoash that he should have struck the ground five or six times. Now he would only get partial victory for that was the only space he had made in his mind.

The verse that follows his altercation with the king simply says, 'Elisha died and was buried.'

When I was a child the author I loved to read more than any other was Charles Dickens. My father bought me a set of his works and I devoured them avidly. I loved the characters and especially the way he used words to such great effect.

There is a poignant moment in the book *Oliver Twist* –
a novel set in a Victorian workhouse. The ragged urchins
are all orphans. There could hardly be a more powerful
metaphor for powerlessness than the picture Dickens
paints. The children are diminutive in stature, frail in
body and without parents to protect them. The Beadle
who controls the workhouse, in contrast, appears to
them, at least, to be all powerful.

At every meagre mealtime the same procedure is performed. Hungry boys, having been given inadequate
rations, shuffle away from their benches with empty
stomachs.

One day the routine is spectacularly broken as the
nine-year-old Oliver takes his empty bowl in his hands
and approaches the towering frame of the Beadle. The
oxygen must have been sucked from the room as
orphans and staff inhale, aghast at such audacity.
Bellowing down at him the Beadle asks what the small
boy wants. With moist supplicating eyes Oliver simply
says 'Please Sir, I want more.'

As he proffers the empty bowl he exhibits before him
the space he longs grace to fill.

We are not urchins coming before a miserly workhouse manager. We are children approaching a loving
father. Someone who is often more willing to give than
we are to receive.

The Apostle Paul praying over the church in Ephesus
articulates a portrait of a God who has offered his grace
to all those will provide the space for it. The passage is
presented below in full. You may find it helpful to read
it through once and then, as we discussed in a previous
chapter, meditate on it until its promise becomes your
own. Might I encourage you also to note the words connected with both space and largeness and, as you
engage with this, I believe that you will experience a

powerful sense of growth and expansiveness in your spirit.

> I pray that out of his glorious riches he may strengthen you with power through his Spirit in your inner being, so that Christ may dwell in your hearts through faith. And I pray that you, being rooted and established in love, may have power, together with all the saints, to grasp how wide and long and high and deep is the love of Christ, and to know this love that surpasses knowledge—that you may be filled to the measure of all the fullness of God.
>
> Now to him who is able to do immeasurably more than all we ask or imagine, according to his power that is at work within us, to him be glory in the church and in Christ Jesus throughout all generations, for ever and ever! Amen.[8]

7

Stepping Up

When arriving at a friends' home for a meal we were ushered into the lounge to find the family's small son engrossed in his PlayStation. When asked to say hello and greet us he responded, with eyes firmly glued on the TV screen before him, 'Hang on Dad, I will in a second, I'm just about to go to the next level!'

In a few years' time he may be saying the same things about his golf handicap or about his progress in his chosen career. I certainly hope so.

Bigger People by definition want to grow to the next level. Their motivation is not mercenary and they do not see themselves in competition with anybody else. It's just that they believe that God has not designated them for stagnation. He has called them to bring forth fruit – fruit that will last.

The sense of being lifted higher occurred at the point we first made a commitment to Christ but should never end there. In an Old Testament context, the psalmist puts it this way:

> I waited patiently for the LORD; he turned to me and heard my cry. He lifted me out of the slimy pit, out of the mud and mire; he set my feet on a rock and gave me a

firm place to stand. He put a new song in my mouth, a hymn of praise to our God. Many will see and fear and put their trust in the LORD.[1]

God takes us out of something – a pit – puts us on to something – a rock – and puts something into us – a song.

To grasp the concept of moving from weakness to strength we are going to look at four of the most vulnerable creatures in God's creation and then at three biblical characters who each, in different ways, experienced a period of vulnerability in their personal lives.

> Four things on earth are small, yet they are extremely wise: Ants are creatures of little strength, yet they store up their food in the summer; conies are creatures of little power, yet they make their home in the crags; locusts have no king, yet they advance together in ranks; a lizard can be caught with the hand, yet it is found in kings' palaces.[2]

The Ant

The ant is an amazing creature. One of the most captivating books on this remarkable insect is, *The Earth Dwellers* by Eric Hoyt.[3] Their colonies are virtually a factory within a fortress and consists of a variety of ants all bred to fulfil a specific duty. They comprise soldiers, builders farmers and nurses. The ant whose sole responsibility is to operate as a leaf-cutter, is able to carry one and a half times its own body weight. All function in a single-minded dedication to the survival of the Queen without which they would lose all purpose. Small wonder the Scripture encourages us to 'Go to the ant . . . consider its ways and be wise!'[4]

Though one of the most vulnerable of all creatures it remains alive through an innate ability to work collectively in preparation for a future when its existence may well be threatened. That is should survive at all is a miracle.

Most of us only notice these insects as they scurry around our gardens and would have little idea how sophisticated their networks are.

The *formica yessensis* ant, for instance, that lives on the Ishikari coast of Hokkaido, Japan reside in forty-five thousand interconnected nests across a square mile and have 306 million workers.

When one compares this with some Christians who live from Sunday to Sunday with virtually no concept of dreams, desires or ambitions to achieve greater things for God, we begin to understand why God has set these creatures as a model.

In his provocative book *Breakout Churches* T.S. Rainer tells us that currently it takes eighty-five church members twelve months to lead one person to Christ and that less than fifteen per cent of Christians have shared their faith with a non-Christian in the past year.[5] The Church clearly has a huge unemployment problem.

An industrious church should be working while it has the opportunity. The Scriptures warn us of a winter which may come in the form of reduced health, limited opportunity or increased persecution. Jesus parallels the theme in the gospels when he speaks of working while it is day in the knowledge that a night approaches when none can work.[6]

The Coney

Some call it the rock badger and it compensates for its smallness by climbing to positions of safety. The Bigger

People concept is not just about growth – it has to do with the willingness to be honest enough to acknowledge those areas of weakness and insecurities that all of us have in our lives and work towards compensating for them by climbing.

When Nehemiah examined the walls of Jerusalem, his priority was to repair the obvious breaches in the defences before he reinforced the areas of the wall that were already in place. While work was done on renovation he supplied the workers with swords as well as trowels. He knew that restoration takes time and we remain vulnerable even while we are working on areas of our lives. All disciples carry L-plates and are 'works in progress'. None of us have 'arrived' spiritually and if anyone thinks that they have they are in the most precarious position of all.[7]

I have long since come to the conclusion that everybody is dealing with insecurities in their life. The only difference is that some people manage to hide the fact better than others.

The Locust

The locust is often used as an analogy for judgement and destruction. In reality they are far more than a metaphor. They can swarm in a cloud containing millions and totally devastate a harvest. Individually they are weak and vulnerable and have little capacity even for directing their own flight. By keeping together, however, they have the capacity to bring an agricultural economy to its knees.

Bigger People recognising their innate weakness climb like the coney to a higher plane. Similarly, the locust joins with others on their journey from struggle to strength.

On a personal basis this could mean that people dealing with the challenge of addiction might identify with a programme like *Teen Challenge* which has brought empowerment and change to tens of thousands of people. Coming under the care of experienced leaders is the attitude of the coney. Working together with others in a similar situation is the wisdom of the locust.

On a church basis this may mean smaller churches in a city linking with others to perform in evangelism or community action. It also may involve larger congregations linking with those who have a different skill set – even if the needed expertise is to be found in a congregation of a smaller size.

The Lizard

Some translations say spider but the principle is the same. The cleanest homes cannot keep out the spider. It will be sure to find a route in for, though weak, its compensating strength is its tenacity.

At 7 p.m. on 20 October 1968 a few thousand spectators still remained in the Olympic stadium in Mexico. An hour earlier, Mamo Wolde of Ethiopia had won the 26 miles 385 yards marathon. Then a lone figure approached the gates. It was J.S. Akhwari. His leg bloodied and bandaged by a fall, he hobbled around the 400 metre track. He finished in exhaustion and was questioned as to why he had not just simply pulled into the side of the road when it was clear that he could not hope to end up with the leaders. He replied, 'My country did not send me seven thousand miles to start a race. They sent me seven thousand miles to finish it.'

Working like the ant, climbing like the coney, uniting with others in similar struggle is important. However, few things carry us from weakness to strength more than the quality of tenacity.

It is said that there were moments when Columbus on his journey to discover a new world was threatened with mutiny. Day after day when the crew realised that there was still no sight of land and, even if they turned back they were likely to starve before reaching home, he faced angry confrontation. When we examine the ship's log during that period we might expect to find a diarist's account of the débâcle that included names, times and incidents. The fact is all that Columbus wrote each day during that period were two words – 'sailed on'.

Having looked at how the Scriptures illustrate the need to compensate for smallness and weakness through the analogy of animals, it's time to turn to three characters who faced a tipping point in their experience which catapulted them into a higher level of encounter with God. Had the moment been missed, these people may have been totally erased from the biblical hall of fame in which they are now enshrined.

David

Goliath was by no means the only giant that David had to face in his life. Given the lack of affirmation he received from his family, his rise to prominence is a miracle in itself.

When God told Samuel to go to Jesse's house because one of his sons was destined to be king he expected to discover someone among the seven sons that were introduced to him. God had already informed the prophet about the criteria he should use.

In the opening chapter we looked at the danger of measuring a tree from the ground up. Bigness, in God's economy has nothing to do with physical, social or financial stature.

'The LORD does not look at the things that man looks at. Man looks at the outward appearance but the LORD looks at the heart.'[8]

It was only when Jesse was pressed that he remembered David and it was not going to be the last time the lad was overlooked.

Some time later when his older brothers were in the armed forces and facing the Philistines, David was requested to take some bread, cheese and wine to them. It was on that errand that he first heard Goliath's taunts and wanted to know who among them was going to take up the challenge.

Eliab, who was still smarting from the rejection of seeing his kid brother receive an anointing that perhaps he had hoped would be his, could stand it no longer:

> When Eliab, David's oldest brother, heard him speaking with the men, he burned with anger at him and asked, "Why have you come down here? And with whom did you leave those few sheep in the desert? I know how conceited you are and how wicked your heart is; you came down only to watch the battle."[9]

A lot of damage can be inflicted in a few short sentences. A smaller person could have been demoralised by the attack on his character, his motive and his integrity. David allowed the fiery darts to glance off him. He may have been more diminutive in size but he was far bigger in spiritual stature than his brother.

All the authority figures in David's life had chosen to dismiss him. His father had initially overlooked him and, as far as the battle was concerned, saw him of no more value than the purveyor of cheese sandwiches.

His brother had impugned his character and later the king, a man who was head and shoulders taller than anyone in Israel, would say the limiting words, 'You are not able . . . you are only a boy'.[10]

What a confusion of giants!

It was at the point that Goliath taunted David with the ultimate put-down, that David revealed the secret of his personal security.

Perhaps as Eliab had been previously speaking David had thought of the meaning of his brother's name – God is my father – and was looking to a higher reference of affirmation than Eliab, in whose imposing shadow he currently stood.

Now to Goliath he says, 'You come against me with sword and spear and javelin, but I come against you in the name of the LORD Almighty, the God of the armies of Israel, whom you have defied.'[11]

The Bible says that the name of the Lord is a strong tower and that the righteous run to it and are safe.[12] It was as if, in that tower, David had raced to the top floor in his confidence of God and now, rather than looking up at a giant, was looking down on him.

There is a huge lesson here for those who aspire to be Bigger People. If we accept the views that others have of us we will be permanently confined to the straitjacket of their limitations on our lives. This is why the Bible says that the fear of man sets a snare and the fear of the Lord is the beginning of wisdom.[13]

Philistines throwing parties should beware of Samsons leaning on pillars – and Goliaths throwing challenges should be aware of Davids rising to their destiny.

Why not pause right now to make a statement. It may well become the bedrock of your future growth. You may find it helpful to speak it out loud so you can hear it, God can hear it and even the devil can hear it. It might also be a good idea to write it on a postcard and pin it above your desk, or keep it in your wallet.

> *I'm stepping up because I have a destiny. No weapon formed against me will prosper. I will allow no one to kill my vision. No one will destroy my dream.*

Deborah

One of the biggest areas of rejection that goes on in the Church is not that which is perpetrated by others but a rejection that we inflict on ourselves. It occurs when two tell-tale words are used – 'if only'. If only I were younger, older, more educated, more extrovert: the list is inexhaustible.

What we are saying is that we are rejecting what we could be because of what we believe that we are.

Deborah could have said, 'If only I weren't a woman,' but thankfully she didn't.

When the angel visited Mary and said that she would bear a son, her initial response was, 'How can this be, since I do not know a man?'[14] It was an understandable response. In all of human history a virgin birth had never occurred before. We can hardly blame Mary for her retort.

What we cannot countenance in the twenty-first century is the assumption that nothing of real value can be accomplished unless a man is involved in it.

I am well are of the controversy that swirls around the Church when headship is mentioned. Those who know me would be aware that I am not a feminist given that I believe firmly in male headship both in the Church and in the home.

I also believe strongly in women leadership and in their ordination to ministry.

A plethora of books have been written on the subject all of which claim divine authority for their opposing points of view. I can well remember, however, the moment of stark simplicity when my own mind was made up on the matter.

As a young man I was aware of people I respected refusing to consider the possibility of women in leadership or preaching to groups that included men in the congregation. I was also totally bemused therefore by hearing them ask us to pray for and support women who had been sent out, sometimes totally alone, to the mission field. It seemed both incongruous and illogical. I was forced to the conclusion that those who embraced such theological dissonance had either to be sexist or racist. There were no other options. Truth had to be universal. Truth cannot be true in one part of the world and false in another.

When Mary argued that God's promise could not come to pass without the involvement of a man, the response of the angel is significant. He put an end to her anxiety with the words 'The Holy Spirit will come upon you, and the power of the Highest will overshadow you.'

The same solution works today for all of us – men and women given challenges by God that initially can seem impossible to carry out, given our personal limitations.

We saw when we considered David that bigness is not be defined by physical stature. Now we are to discover that authority is not defined by the designation of status or title.

There were two significant men in Deborah's life. One was her husband Lappidoth (fiery torch) and the other was her military commander Barak (lightning).

On learning this one immediately thinks of the words God speaks to the church in Sardis when he told them that they had a name for being alive but were in fact spiritually dead.[15]

Status does not necessarily carry with it greatness and influence is a great deal more important than mere institutional power.

The story is told of a farmer who was approached by a pinstriped official demanding access to one of his fields. When the farmer expressed forcibly that he would not advise it the civil servant countered the rebuff by brandishing a dossier of papers above his head with the cry, 'I must have access because I have brought with me the necessary authority.'

The farmer reluctantly gave way and the official pushed passed him brusquely. It was only then that the man realised that he was now in the presence of a snorting bull and as it chased him over the grass the farmer was heard to shout after him, 'Why not show him your authority!'

The Church is very good at declaring its authority but sometimes something less than competent in exercising it. As evangelicals we are quick to raise our Bible aloft and declare that we believe it all. The world sometimes looks on in bewilderment as it witnesses some areas of our spiritual impotence and understandably asks, 'Where is it all?'

It was words that had taunted David but facts taunted Deborah.

After her momentous victory had been secured we are blessed with what has become known as her song – part of which gives us a glimpse of both her motivation and her source of strength:

> When the people willingly offer themselves—praise the
> LORD . . . life in Israel ceased, ceased until I, Deborah,

arose, arose a mother in Israel . . . may those who love you be like the sun when it rises in its strength.[16]

Deborah did not accomplish her victory simply because of ineffectual men around her. Deborah rose to her destiny because, as the Scripture records, 'she arose a mother in Israel like 'the sun when it rises in its strength' – coming to a gradual yet increasing awareness that God could use her despite the contrary views of others around her.

The message is not that women arise in situations in which men appear not up to the challenge. The solution to a Church, that desires to grow in greatness and influence, is strong and anointed men and women simultaneously making themselves available to fulfil the purposes of God in their generation.

If you are a woman who is reading this chapter, the following declaration can become your own:

> *I am stepping up and moving away from any reluctance to fulfil God's call upon my life. Like Mary I believe the Spirit of God will overshadow me as I make myself available to be a carrier of Christ into my community. Like Deborah I refuse to be intimidated by the prejudices of others. My hope is in the Lord and he will make my paths straight and ensure that his purposes succeed through my character, my intellect, my personality and my gifts.*

Gideon

How does a man move from being a wimp to being a warrior?

David did not say 'If only I weren't so young.' Deborah did not say 'If only I weren't a woman.' And eventually Gideon did not say 'If only I weren't in such a mess.' I say 'eventually' because, in Gideon's case, as in so many of our own lives, change comes more often through process than crisis.

Crisis was something that Gideon knew about – living as he did in a nation surrounded by enemies who tantalisingly waited for harvest time before destroying their crops. When the angel arrives to bring him a message he finds him threshing wheat in a wine press. He was there because this was the last place the Midianites expected to find anyone. Rejoicing and celebration were forgotten experiences in a nation where people had been driven from their own homes and were living in caves.

The greeting that the angelic visitor brought could hardly have been more crushing – for like Lappidoth and Barak, Gideon, whose name means mighty warrior, also had a name to which he was failing to measure up to.

Yet this is how the angel addressed him. In the same way that Jesus called Peter a rock before he made him one, the appellation was a declaration of intention. That's the amazing thing about the work of the Holy Spirit in our lives. We see ourselves as we are but God always sees us as we can be. It is at the point that we see through God's eyes rather than our own that things begin to change. That, intrinsically, is what spiritual vision is all about.

When the angel offers him the promise of the presence of God, Gideon, to commence with, is far from convinced:

> "But sir," Gideon replied, "if the LORD is with us, why has all this happened to us? Where are all his wonders that our fathers told us about when they said, 'Did not the LORD bring us up out of Egypt?' But now the LORD has abandoned us and put us into the hand of Midian."[17]

The power of process is possible because God did not simply harangue them when they were living below the level that they should. It would have been so easy for God to do just that. After all, the nation was in this mess as a result of seven years of sin.

It is sometimes less than easy to know, when we are feeling bad about a situation, whether it is the Holy Spirit bringing us under conviction or the devil bringing us under condemnation. There is a simple test. If as a result of what I am feeling I want to give up – then the source is satanic. If as a result of what I am feeling I have a desire to climb higher – the source is most certainly the Holy Sprit. The spiritual physics is simple: the devil wants to drag us down and the Lord always wants to lift us.

Gideon was already in a pit far deeper than the wine press he was actually in and the last thing he needed was a lecture.

If the angel had hovered overhead and reminded him of his sin that would have been an illustration of legalism. If the messenger had stood at a distance and expressed sorrow for his plight that would have been an expression of sympathy. What the angel decided to do was unprecedented. Having come all the way from heaven he gets as close to Gideon as he could and sits down at his level in the ultimate expression of empathy.

It is not our purpose here to catalogue Gideon's journey – only to highlight his first faltering move out of his dilemma. It is a Chinese proverb that says a journey of a thousand miles starts with a single step.

The Lord's word to Gideon was powerful. It was not 'wait until you have got it all together' but rather, 'Go in the strength that you have and deliver Israel.'

You would not have read this far if you did not have a heart to grow higher and deeper in spiritual stature.

However, if like Gideon you are not only aware of your own frailty but also of a sense of failure, those powerful words have the potency to turn your life around if you will allow them to.

It was J.M. Barrie who once said, 'We are all failures; at least, the best of us are.'[18]

The answer to why God uses people who have failed in the past is that there is nobody else to use. Superman and superwoman do not live here anymore.

After the medieval St Paul's Cathedral had burned down in the Great Fire of London, Christopher Wren was the architect commissioned to rebuild it. It was a massive undertaking and prior to putting pen to paper he went out to wander among the ruins. As he walked amidst the tragic scene of devastation his foot stumbled against some rubble. Looking closer he discovered that the fallen masonry against which he had tripped was part of an inscription relating to the Easter story. Four compelling words met his gaze – and nine years later the building stood proud and tall. The four words were, 'I will rise again.'

Have dreams fallen at your feet? Has hope been razed to the ground? Before you are tempted to capitulate to circumstances listen, in your spirit, to the words found in Micah:

> Do not gloat over me, my enemy! Though I have fallen, I will rise. Though I sit in darkness, the LORD will be my light. Because I have sinned against him, I will bear the LORD's wrath, until he pleads my case and establishes my right. He will bring me out into the light; I will see his righteousness.[19]

Here is a prayer that you might like to offer:

> *Father of compassion, thank you that in your mercy you have called me to yourself. Thank you that your grace has relentlessly*

pursued me. Though I have failed you have never let me down and you have promised to never let me go. You have also said that, even when I fall, I will not be utterly cast down, for you uphold me with your hand. I will rise again. I will go in the strength that I have. I will grow deeper and climb higher as your continued presence enables me. In your strength I will fulfil your desire for my life.

Epilogue

The term 'building Bigger People' came into my spirit in 1999 just after my election to the office of General Superintendent for the Elim Pentecostal Churches. I knew immediately that this would be a primary principle that would underpin the vision and values that I, and my team, would seek to disseminate throughout the Movement during our period of service.

The catalyst was an account that I had read of George Mallory's attempt to climb Everest. Up until that time no one had ever climbed higher that 24,600 feet. His remains were found in 1999 at 27,000 feet where they had lain encased in ice and snow for seventy-five years.

Giving a lecture after Mallory's death on the mountain in 1924, one of the expedition concluded his talk by pointing to a picture of the yet-unconquered peak with the words 'We tried to beat you and we failed. We tried again and you beat us. But we will conquer you for you cannot grow bigger, but we can.'[1]

In 1953 the New Zealander Edmund Hillary and the Nepalese sherpa Tenzing Norgay became the first to reach the summit of Mount Everest.

The Church is destined to conquer. If it is to do so in our generation it must be willing to climb. To climb, it has to grow Bigger People – those who can believe that God can accomplish great things through them. They must not succumb to the altitude sickness that condemns them to smallness. Nothing must hold them back – not age, gender, personal frailty or even past failure.

I believe that this can be your experience today: the destiny for which you have been created.

Notes

1. The Flavour of Favour

[1] Deut. 32:15
[2] Mk. 6:5,6
[3] Ex. 23:30
[4] Eph. 2:8
[5] 1 Sam. 2:19
[6] 1 Sam. 2:26
[7] Song 2:4
[8] Mt. 23:37
[9] Gen. 6:8
[10] Lk. 2:14
[11] Ps. 5:12
[12] Ps. 84:11
[13] Lk. 4:18,19
[14] Deut. 33:23

2. The Four-faced Church

[1] Dan. 7:4 & Rev. 4:7
[2] Ex. 33:18,19
[3] Ps. 19:1

[4] Jn. 2:11
[5] Jn. 17:5
[6] Is. 55:9
[7] Is. 22:1
[8] Rom. 8:28
[9] 1 Sam. 30:6
[10] Ps. 69:6
[11] 1 Cor. 10:12 (Amplified Bible)
[12] Ex. 4:21–26
[13] Judg. 18:27
[14] Gen. 10:15
[15] 2 Cor. 1:24
[16] Gal. 5:13
[17] Lk. 19:10
[18] Lk. 7:47
[19] Mt. 5:16
[20] Hab. 2:14
[21] Heb. 13:3
[22] Mt. 16:18

3. A Bigger Voice

[1] 2 Kgs. 4
[2] Neh. 6:3
[3] Prov. 29:25
[4] Ps. 137
[5] Rom. 8:26
[6] Mt. 14:30
[7] Rev. 22:18,19
[8] Acts 8:29
[9] Heb. 2:18
[10] Ps. 66:18
[11] Prov. 28:9
[12] Jas. 4:3

13 1 Cor. 3:13

14 Prov. 21:13

15 Phil. 4:12

16 1 Pet. 5:5

17 Watchman Nee, *The Spiritual Man* (Anaheim: Living Stream Ministry, 1998).

18 John Maxwell, *Failing Forward* (Nashville: Thomas Nelson, 2000).

19 Ex. 38:8

20 1 Pet. 3:7

21 My paraphrase of Mt. 6:14

22 C.S. Lewis, *Weight of Glory* (Grand Rapids: Zondervan, 2001).

23 1 Sam. 3:19–21

4. Generational Blessing

1 Ps. 119:105

2 Gen. 3:15

3 Rev. 21:5 (KJV)

4 Dan. 7:9

5 Ex. 16:32

6 Gen. 11:31,32

7 1 Thes. 1:6, 1 Thes. 2:7 and 1 Thes. 2:11

8 1 Cor. 4:15–17 (NKJV)

9 Gen. 20

10 Gen. 12:11–13

11 Gen. 26:9

12 2 Tim. 1:5,6

13 Ps. 45:16,17

5. The Home of the Heart

[1] John Flavel, *The Mystery of Providence* (Edinburgh: Banner of Truth, 1963).
[2] Ps. 113:7–9
[3] 1 Sam. 2:8
[4] Mk. 10:51 (KJV)
[5] Acts 19
[6] Michael L. Brown, *From Holy Laughter to Holy Fire* (Carlisle: STL, 1997).
[7] Mk. 6:11,12
[8] Is. 26:19
[9] Acts 13:51,52
[10] Is. 52
[11] Ps. 51:6
[12] Ps. 133 (NKJV)
[13] Lk. 12:3 (NKJV)
[14] Prov. 28:1
[15] Jer. 17:9
[16] Eph. 5:27

6. Space for Grace

[1] Mt. 9:29
[2] 2 Kgs. 3:11–14
[3] 2 Kgs. 3:15
[4] 1 Cor. 6:12 (Amplified Bible)
[5] Mk. 11:3
[6] Lk. 16:8
[7] 2 Kgs. 13
[8] Eph. 6:16–21

7. Stepping Up

1   Ps. 40:1–3
2   Prov. 30:24–28
3   Eric Hoyt, *The Earth Dwellers* (London: Simon & Schuster, 1996).
4   Prov. 6:6
5   T.S. Rainer, *Breakout Churches* (Grand Rapids: Zondervan, 2005).
6   Jn. 9:4
7   1 Cor. 10:12
8   1 Sam. 16:7
9   1 Sam. 17:28
10   1 Sam. 17:33
11   1 Sam. 17:45
12   Prov. 18:10
13   Prov. 29:25 & Ps. 111:10
14   Lk. 1:34 (NKJV)
15   Rev. 3:1
16   Judg. 5
17   Judg. 6:13,14
18   J.M. Barrie quotation found on www.quoteworld.org, original source unknown.
19   Mich. 7:8,9

Epilogue

1   Source unknown